Curious Creatures
of New England

Disclaimer: The purpose of this book is to share stories regarding the paranormal experiences people have encountered cryptids, wild creatures of unknown origin at the time they were spotted. The stories are meant to entertain and narrate traditional tales, urban legends, hoaxes, wide-held beliefs subject to conjecture, and tales that are downright unexplainable. While the stories are interesting and entertaining, we do not suggest that they are necessarily factual support of the existence of these cryptids…just evidence that we have gathered from multiple sources that describe fascinatingly, and often unexplainable, creatures of New England. Read on and see if you believe in these curious creatures.

Cover Designed by Justin Watkinson
Designed by Matthew Goodman
Type set in Mom's Typewriter/Times

ISBN: 978-0-7643-4466-4

Printed in the United States of America

Published by Schiffer Publishing, Ltd.
4880 Lower Valley Road
Atglen, PA 19310

Phone: (610) 593-1777; Fax: (610) 593-2002
E-mail: Info@schifferbooks.com
For the largest selection of fine reference books
on this and related subjects, please visit our website at
www.schifferbooks.com.

You may also write for a free catalog.
This book may be purchased from the publisher.
Please try your bookstore first.
We are always looking for people to write books on new and related subjects.
If you have an idea for a book, please contact us at proposals@schifferbooks.com

Schiffer Books are available at special discounts for bulk purchases for sales promotions or premiums. Special editions, including personalized covers, corporate imprints, and excerpts can be created in large quantities for special needs. For more information contact the publisher.

Curious Creatures
of New England

Christopher Forest

4880 Lower Valley Road • Atglen, PA 19310

Dedication

This book is dedicated to my wonderful wife, Melissa, who continues to be my dedicated photographer, resident historical expert, idea bouncer, and beautiful spouse. She has shared in these stories too often to tell.

Melissa, I couldn't have done this book without you.

Acknowledgments

I would like to thank Brighid and Christopher who have to put up with their father and his incessant jaunts to new places to find fun and exciting information for these books. Also, a special thanks to my family who have heard and took part in these tales during the course of many years, especially to my parents, brother, and sister who instilled an interest in curious creatures at a very early age. And finally, a special thanks to friends I had growing up, such as Scott, Rob, and Prasad, who helped me pursue learning more about unique and unusual creatures. It seems as if it has been a part of my life forever.

Thanks to all of you!

Contents

Foreword

The stories contained in this book are a composite of many tales told throughout the years. They attempt to capture a glimpse of unusual creatures that have been spotted in New England during the course of at least three centuries. Some of the stories have long been told, while others are more recent. Some have lengthy stories behind them, while others have become more like contemporary urban legends. Most of the stories are based on fact and lore, while a few might be more of a fantastic fabrication. Whatever the source, this book examines the unique blend of cryptid tales that permeate New England.

I intend to share these cryptid tales from New England's past and present. In some cases, the information might point to the fact that earthly—and not supernatural—sources are the true cause of an unsolved mystery.

Many of the places that are mentioned in this book still exist. Some have vanished into history, while others no longer have the access that they may have once enjoyed. A variety of spots that were once open to the public are now businesses or private buildings. Some of the islands that are mentioned no longer allow visitors, and the cemeteries listed here have strict visiting rules.

Paranormal and cryptid enthusiasts are a fun group. However, we ask that if you decide to learn more about these places for yourself, you respect the privacy of those places that have now turned into businesses, residences, or private properties, as well as respect the rules of the islands and cemeteries that dot New England. This, too, is not an endorsement to go looking for cryptid creatures; that is best left up to cryptozoologists.

Incidentally, the chapter about the sea serpent of the North Shore has been reprinted—in part—from a version that appears in my book *North Shore Spirits of Massachusetts*.

Please enjoy the *Curious Creatures of New England.*

Introduction

New England has long been a wonderful region of America, filled with tradition, filled with culture, and filled with history. It is a region that helped give birth to the United States and has helped developed some of the most interesting episodes in American history. Some of that history is well known, but other elements of that history...well, they remain hidden.

Part of that history includes strange tales of the unknown. The earlier settlers to the region, Native Americans, told these tales and then passed them on to future generations. Historians have suggested the tales of the wild, and a general lack of knowledge of the landscape, helped fuel an early New England fear of the supernatural. As European settlers arrived, they learned of these stories, retold them, and added a few of their own. Many have withstood the test of time and remain a fabric of New England today.

Part of the magical folklore of the region includes a variety of stories about creatures that roam the backwoods and hillsides of New England. From the White Mountains, to the lakes of the Massachusetts, to the coasts of Maine, and Southern New England, tales abound of the odd, the strange, and the sublime: Hairy beasts that remind us of Bigfoot, large sea monsters that swallow ships whole, and mythical creatures that taunt any passersby.

Come and enjoy the tales in this collection of cryptid encounters. It is presented as an encyclopedia, of sorts, to narrate the various creatures found in New England. Putting it together took more doing than I thought. In fact, my first venture probably dates back to sixth grade, when, for a science fair project, I actually wrote a report called, "Man, Mysteries, and Monsters." From those humble beginnings began the first incarnation of this book.

Finding information about the amazing creatures of the region took some time, some effort, and some detours through dead-ends...but the stories I found were simply a joy. Some are more fabled than fact while others will have you wondering just what might be around the bend, so, the next time you are in New England, remember to pause and take a look—that shadow you see just might be one of New England's curious creatures.

Ascutney Alligator

Location: Ascutney, Vermont
Type of Creature: Giant reptile or lizard
Last Seen: 1960s

The History

Ascutney is a quaint region on Vermont's eastern border with New Hampshire. It is a quiet section, known for its state park, with scenic vistas and rivers for canoeing. Visitors flock to this part of the state in the fall, watching the sky light up in the colors of autumn. Festivals and harvest fairs help visitors transcend to another time.

The Mystery

Ascutney State Park is also the site of a unique cryptid sighting from the 1960s. According to authors Joseph Citro and Bonnie Christiansen in *Green Mountain Ghosts, Ghouls, and Unsolved Mysteries*, in 1968, tourists in the region encountered something a little out of the ordinary.

The story originally came from press clippings. The *United Press* ran an article about a strange encounter in the waters of the park. According to the report, Douglas and Dorothy Grove of Manchester, New Hampshire, were enjoying a pleasant day in the waters of the state park's lake. While canoeing through one of the more peaceful parts of the Connecticut River, they noticed a peculiar animal passing close to their canoe. While peculiar creatures are not uncommon in the waters of New England—beavers and otters are often seen, particularly at night, appearing suddenly and uniquely in the water—this was no ordinary animal. The creature that swam near them seemed to be an odd reptile-type with green scales. They theorized that it was one-and-one-half to two feet long and weighed, at most, two pounds.

The Groves reported the sighting to local authorities. While the officials did search the area, they found nothing out of the ordinary. What was the creature? A runaway 'gator? An escaped lizard? No one knows. Since that day, the creature has never been reported again...but there is little doubt that something a bit out of the ordinary was swimming in the Connecticut River back in 1968. To this day, that creature is lovingly known as the "Ascutney Alligator."

Ap'cnic Water Monster

Location: Littleton, Massachusetts
Type of Creature: Giant squid
Last Seen: Unknown

The History

The waters of Nagog Pond in Littleton, Massachusetts, have served as the town reservoir for Concord since 1909. A small body of water, the pond is owned by the town and kept secure. However, at one time, the region was the home of the Nashoba Praying Indian Village. Constructed with the help of Reverend John Elliot, a noted minister to Native Americans, the village was the sixth of fourteen such villages in Massachusetts predicated on teaching Native Americans Christianity.

The Mystery

While the pond serves as a reservoir, it is also home to a unique mystery. According to some Native American legends, the pond has long been the home of Ap'cnic, a water monster, which some might say best resembles the giant squid in Walt Disney's *20 Thousand Leagues Under the Sea.*

The monster is best described by writer John Mitchell in the book *Trespassing.* According to his research, the creature was large, had horns, and a large beak that was known to ascend from the water, searching for victims. Its long, tentacled arms would ply the shore for prey. Once found, Ap'cnic pulled its victim into the water, and then mashed it to pieces with its beak.

Exactly where this legend developed is still subject to debate. However, the region around the pond has long been considered a home of supernatural forces. The Nashoba Native Americans believed that a nearby hill actually contained the four winds that would, at times, surface from the area, causing other nearby hills to quake. An earthquake was even registered in the area in the 1980s, adding to the mystery of the spot.

Bigfoot of New England

The History

He's tall. He's hairy. And he is one heck of an ugly fellow. No, he is not your average creature. He's Bigfoot…and he just may be alive and well in New England. When most people think of Bigfoot, they think of the classic creature lumbering through the woods. Most people picture him silhouetted against an over-arching background of pine or sequoia trees. Northwest Pacific at its finest. Or perhaps, even the northern regions of the southeast.

New England is not your stereotypical Bigfoot country. However, it has had some classic cases of Bigfoot creatures spotted throughout the years. In fact, it is probably a hidden gem among Sasquatch enthusiasts, and, when you consider the abundant forests and lush vegetations found throughout the region, particularly the northern sections, you can see why Bigfoot might have a home in the area.

Bigfoot researchers are quick to point out that Bigfoot has been classically spotted in all states of New England except for Rhode Island. To most cryptid enthusiasts, it appears the Ocean State has never had an official Bigfoot sighting—however, there are sightings of Bigfoot-like creatures in the region, which make it highly likely that if Bigfoot is in New England, than he might not be that far from the Newport shores.

According to the Bigfoot Field Research Organization (BFRO), Bigfoot sightings have been reported in the area as far back as the mid-eighteenth century. During the period of the French and Indian War, many settlers explored—and attacked—through the backwoods of the country, more than likely setting a few Bigfoot into motion.

Why would Bigfoot come to such a congested area? Well, the reason is quite simple. There are thousands upon thousands of untouched acres that a Bigfoot clan could claim as territory without ever worrying about the day-to-day encounters with humans. Of course, this has not stopped people from spotting Bigfoot here or there. In fact, the region seems rife with many encounters.

Below, you will find a list of the encounters by state and some interesting, and perhaps even startling, stories from an encounter in at least each state.

The Mystery

Maine:
Baxter State Park

Maine may be the home of lobsters, outlet stores, and rocky beaches. Yet, it is also the home of many Bigfoot sightings. The BFRO has registered at least ten reports throughout the region of these encounters.

One of the more interesting ones occurred in Baxter State Park in 1970. The state park is a true Maine treasure. Tourists and nature lovers alike often go to the park to enjoy the scenery, a hike up Mt. Katahdin, or the scenic waterways nearby. However, in 1970, a scientist on a hunting expedition met more than he bargained for in the park. While roaming the woods, he came across some foul-smelling scat that had been left behind by some animal. The aroma hung heavy in the air, calling the scientist's attention to a nearby pile of dung.

He looked at the dung and noticed that it was about a foot-long, the size of a good-sized human remains after a late-night eating binge. The scientist became wary that someone else might also be in the woods. There was a peculiar feeling gnawing at him. The quiet of the woods bothered him. The eerie silenced was punctured by the sound of loud thumping. Suddenly, a giant tree came crashing down in front of his path—not too far from where he was standing. The man believed the tree came down with a little assistance from something else.

Needless to say, the man took off into the woods, but, as a true scientist might do, he returned the following day with a friend. They walked into the swampy woodland, hoping to investigate more. Their investigation was cut short when they entered a rocky region, which they realized could pose a challenge if a wild creature was indeed in the area. Just as they prepared to turn back, the quiet of the day was again interrupted by a loud thumping noise. Before they knew it, a giant boulder flew over their heads and landed nearby. The two men didn't need to think twice…they took off from the area before anything else could happen.

According to the *bigfootencounters* website, sightings of the creature near Baxter State Park are not an uncommon phenomenon. Some sources suggest that local Native American tribes recounted tales of meeting strange human-like creatures several centuries ago in the region.

The site also mentions another, more recent encounter with a Bigfoot-type creature. A report on the site highlights a strange encounter of a family that was a regular visitor to the region. While visiting the park and the nearby town of Millinocket, the family chanced upon some hikers who invited them to their camp.

While chatting, a strange, shrill cry, like that of a bird, interrupted the quiet. While the family thought nothing of it at the time, one of the hikers joked that the creature of Mt. Katahdin must have been out and about.

The family, who had visited the region for nearly a decade, had never heard of these strange tales of Katahdin creatures. Little did they know the wild tale would soon take a turn for the surreal.

Later that night, the family visited the hikers again at their campsite. As the hours turned late, the family heard a strange noise in the woods. The campsite was then pelted by stones. The campers flicked on a nearby camping light, only to be startled by a strange creature shielding itself from the light.

According to the report, the campers saw a large, hairy man-like creature (or, perhaps, even a hairy man), covered with a thick red fur coat of some sort. The creature stared at them momentarily, then moved on. Frozen in curiosity and a little bit of fear, the campers returned to their tents and investigated the following day. They found no trace of a strange creature— or an overly-hairy man—and never quite knew what they saw.

Massachusetts: October Mountain

October Mountain is the site of a picturesque state park in Massachusetts. Nestled in a portion of the Appalachian Mountains known as the Berkshires, the park is a popular spot with outdoorsmen and tourists. The park is home to a portion of the Appalachian trail as well as the potential home of a possible Bigfoot.

Several sightings of the hairy beast have occurred in the region. Perhaps the most well-known sightings occurred in the 1980s. According to the the North East Sasquatch Researchers Association (NESRA) website, in 1983, two men and two women reported an encounter with a creature that closely resembled the classic Bigfoot profile.

One night, the foursome was camping, supposedly, near an abandoned Boy Scout camp that had once been open in the area. While sitting around a fire enjoying a cookout, they began to hear strange noises in the woods at about 10 p.m. The noises persisted sporadically for a couple of hours. Finally deciding that the sounds merited investigation, the foursome went for a closer look into the woods when, suddenly, a silhouette caught their eyes. There, about 150 feet masked against the glow of a moon, was an unmistakable appearance of a large, hairy creature. It definitely looked out of place.

Realizing that their campout plans might have to be put on hold, the foursome quickly fled the area in their car. As they pulled out, they swore the car's beams cascaded onto the creature in the woods. The following day, the two men went back to the area for a second look and claimed to have seen the creature fleeing deeper into the overgrowth.

Six years later, in July 1989, a woman had a potential Bigfoot encounter near October Mountain. While walking on one of the trails, she happened to notice a strange creature moving about in the brush. She paused for a moment, reached for her binoculars, which she had toted along with her, and studied the creature in awe as it roamed the trail.

According to the BFRO, the woman watched as the creature entered a clearing. It began digging into the ground, as if looking for food, and then appeared to be eating something. She moved in for a closer look and realized the creature was, instead, stacking rocks.

It was tall, rather large, and covered with red hair. Its head seemed to be an unusual shape and, at first, the woman thought it might be a human in a costume. She moved closer to look, realizing that this creature might indeed be something special. When the woman was about sixty feet from it, an unsettling feeling came over her. She realized that it might have seen her, and she decided that this encounter was enough for the day.

Whether or not October Mountain is home to a Bigfoot may never be known. However, the region is densely forested. There are many trails that roam through the area, but thick patches of brush and low-lying trees help to mask trails and hide potential inhabitants. There are also many side paths that would offer protection from the elements. Indeed, if a Bigfoot was present in the area, October Mountain would provide a suitable hideaway.

New Hampshire:
The White Mountains

Each year, travelers flock to the White Mountains for its picturesque autumn views, its great day-trip destinations, and its long, windy roads that provide a glimpse of the amazing mountain range in the area. However, those mountains vistas might be hiding more than meets the eye…they might be hiding a potential Bigfoot or two.

Rumors of Bigfoot living in the area have persisted since at least the 1890s. According to local reports, in that decade, a remarkable story unfolded. A man happened to be living in a cabin by Connor Pond, located in the vicinity of Bald and Whittier Mountains. One late winter day, as the ice on the pond began to melt, the man's dog decided to take advantage of the weather. The dog raced onto the pond, only to fall into decaying ice. The man watched as the dog struggled to get out of the ice. Without warning, a sudden crashing sound permeated the nearby woods. The man looked up to see a large creature, covered in hair, walking upright toward the pond. It waded into the pond, reached in, and pulled out the dog. The creature then walked straight toward the vicinity of Bald Mountain, disappearing into the dense woods.

This first official report of a Granite State Bigfoot-like sighting was certainly not the last. Another sighting of the legendary giant occurred in the summer of 1979 when a man named Peter Samuelson, a prospector by hobby, decided to enjoy a day out at Bald Mountain looking for precious minerals. Peter, accompanied by his girlfriend, Holly, and dog, Kat, marched into the woods, intent on finding something of value. What they saw was remarkably different.

While wandering through the woods, they happened to notice a strange cabin not too far from the trail. The cabin, made from stones, with a roof made of hemlock, seemed to be a rudimentary shelter and quite out of place. As they walked closer to the cabin, to within 100 yards of it, they saw that it was occupied by a rather large and hairy creature. They paused a moment to watch it. Samuelson estimated the creature must have been seven feet tall and the fur on the beast was gray, tangled, and had to be nearly three

19

inches long. They watched, astonished, for moments, until Kat became alarmed. Soon, the thing became aware of their presence and began uttering some rather unusual noises. Samuelson, Holly, and Kat did not stay for a second look, but took off down the path they'd come, avoiding a confrontation with whatever it was. It was only later, when they remembered they'd had a camera, that they wished they had taken a picture of it.

A year later, Samuelson returned to the mountain hoping to find some sign of the mysterious creature. Holly refused to go, but Samuelson needed to see if there was something more to the unusual sighting. Once at the top of the mountain, he became quickly dismayed. Nothing remained of the crude structure they had seen before. In fact, there was no noticeable evidence that a structure, or a creature, had actually been seen on the land.

In 2001, a camper in the White Mountains also reported evidence of a possible Bigfoot in the region. While camping during a period of thawing and refreezing, the camper noticed some footprints about eighteen inches in length. Although initially not thinking much about the prints, figuring they must have been made by a local snow-shoer, the camper's mind soon changed. He realized that such marks would have been disrupted by the melting process. The tracks he'd spotted were clearly made by a biped, and in his estimation, had to be made by a large creature that was able to deftly navigate the region *without* snowshoes: a potential Bigfoot.

What exactly lives in the White Mountains may remain a mystery for some time. But ask local folks, and they might tell you to be on the lookout for Bigfoot.

Vermont:
Bennington

Vermont may be the Green Mountain State, but, to local enthusiasts, it also might be the Bigfoot state. Since early times, reports of strange creatures roaming the land have surfaced. One particular hotspot, Bennington, has been forever linked with unusual inhabitants. While it might be the home of the notable monster (see page 66), it also might be the home of the big, hairy guy himself.

The first recorded Bigfoot encounter in the region happened in 1879. On October 18th of that year, two hunters were roaming in the area when they spied what looked like a wild creature near the woods. According to a *New York Times* report from the day, the hunters were stunned when a strange looking creature, about five feet tall, jumped from a boulder. It was covered with red hair, had a long beard, and flashed "wild eyes" in the direction of the hunters.

Surprised, the hunters and the creature came eye-to-eye with one another. One of the hunters pointed a rifle at it and the creature immediately took off toward the woods. The hunter shot at the strange monster and apparently wounded it. It let off several fierce cries, and then, in a fit of rage, took off toward the hunters and began to attack them.

The men quickly ran. They were so scared...they dropped their guns and took off for home, daring not to return for fear of it.

Similar creatures have been spotted over the years. Most of the sightings have occurred during the last few decades. In October of 1976, a woman wandered into the woods, planning to enjoy the peace and quiet of the local forest. While reading a good book beneath the leaves that were gently turning color in the fall air, her solitude was interrupted by a large monster that appeared out of nowhere. According to the woman, the creature stood more than eight feet tall, had broad shoulders, and a large, muscular neck.

Thirteen years later, further evidence to support the existence of a strange creature also surfaced in the region. A man walking in the town of Eden, near Bennington, noticed odd footprints in the woods. Measuring the prints, he noticed that they were almost an out-of-the-ordinary fourteen inches long—longer than the typical native to the region.

In 2003, Ray Dufresne, a resident of nearby Woonsooki, returning from a trip to visit his daughter at Southern Vermont University, found something peculiar along Route 27. According to Dufresne, in a report in the *Bennington Banner* newspaper, he noticed what looked like a strange-looking creature roaming the side of the road.

An avid hunter and sportsmen, Dufresne was intrigued...and then he realized this was no ordinary animal at all. It appeared to be something quite different. The creature seemed tall, and Dufresne assumed it was a person dressed in a gorilla costume. Upon a closer look, though, it looked like no costume he'd ever seen.

Whatever it was appeared to have long arms. It also had long, black hair and did not seem bothered by Dufresne's car. Dufresne thought about turning back, but did not, and shared his story upon returning to town... much to the delight of listeners.

Although Dufresne is familiar with the animals of the Vermont woods, that did not stop local gaming officials from clearly ruling out "Bigfoot" as a possible cause of his sighting. Local officials believed that Dufresne was either confused by a bear walking upright or by a moose appearing out of the woods. Dufresne, however, had been a hunter since 1973 and clearly knew most animals when he saw them. He was certain that the creature was no optical illusion.

Cameos in Connecticut

Connecticut is no exception to the Bigfoot legend. While the number of sightings that have occurred in the Constitution State is much less than in other New England states, there are still quite a few occurrences.

Throughout the last 120 years, stories of a potential Bigfoot have spread throughout the state. The most famous involves the Winstead Wildman (see page 145), though reports of this creature that roamed through the region seem to be based on a hoax. Still, the reports have coincided with a variety of other Bigfoot sightings, which perhaps are based more on reality.

The region near Windham is populated with a variety of Bigfoot sightings. In 1997, a horseback rider reported having a possible Bigfoot encounter in the town of Tomaston. While riding and pausing for a drink, she happened to notice strange, large footprints in the dirt. Puzzled, she became alarmed when an overwhelming, disgusting odor filled the air. Moments later, a large noise erupted in the nearby woods. It sounded like a large animal charging through the forest, crushing branches and undergrowth as it raced toward her.

She quickly evacuated the area on her horse. She never saw what the creature was that was coming at her, but the sound of the footprints barraging through the woods made her decide against staying to find out. She did not even pause for a moment to think about it.

In a swampy region of Barkhamsted National Forest, two young siblings were camping near the swampy area of the forest in 2002. They were enjoying a peaceful scene around the campsite when the solitude was pierced by a sudden sound. Out of the woods, a group of deer emerged. They watched, momentarily, as the deer enjoyed the outskirts of the swamp and then disappeared into the woods.

Seconds later, a strange odor of rotten eggs filled the air. The brothers looked at each other—not sure what to think—and they went about their business. They saw the family of deer off in the distance, erupting from the woods, and then watched as a giant beast gave pursuit. It appeared to be a large, Bigfoot-type in pursuit of a next meal.

The creature caught up with one of the deer and began to attack it. The brothers decided to interrupt the impromptu meal by moving in for a closer look and the Bigfoot became alarmed. It began to growl in their direction. Startled nonetheless, the creature returned to the woods, moving away from the humans.

Rhode Island Bigfoot

For many years, it was believed that Bigfoot had been found in just about every state, except Rhode Island. Was it that the state was too small for Bigfoot? Or perhaps he just wasn't into mansions. Whatever the reason, it seemed Bigfoot strayed far from the Ocean State.

However, it appears that this is simply not true. In recent years, a group has formed the Big Rhodey Research Project (Big Rhodey is the nickname given to Rhode Island's Bigfoot) to search for evidence. It seems that Bigfoot has indeed been spotted in Rhode Island, at least seven times.

Most research has turned up broken trees, clumps of hair, or oversized, human-like prints. However, the most interesting and well-documented experience occurred in 2010. According to a *North Kingstown Patch* article, in October 2011, two bigfoot hunters, Dina Palazini and Kris Stepney, were visiting Exeter, Rhode Island, in search of the creature. During their hunt, they happened to see a creature of some sort wandering in the woods. Acting quickly, they made a short video of the creature as it walked around.

Though the video lasts only a few seconds, and is blurry, it shows what resembles a Bigfoot walking upright through the woods. The creature does appear hunched over, and though hard to recognize in the video, had brown hair and a sloping forehead. It sparked the interest of Bigfoot enthusiasts and even prompted the television network Animal Planet to send a video crew for part of its *Finding Bigfoot* series.

Since that time, Carl Johnson, founder of the Big Rhodey Research Project, has also had a Bigfoot experience. Although he hasn't seen a Bigfoot, he does believe he may have heard one in Cumberland. Practicing a technique called tree-knocking—knocking on trees to communicate with such creatures—a return call was eventually heard...followed by many more calls, getting closer. It sounded like the beast was rushing toward the knocking as a way to scare him off.

Johnson never saw it, though, and the 2010 video taken by Plazini and Stepney only shows a blurry footage of a creature that resembles Bigfoot. Yet, evidence suggests that if Bigfoot does exist, then it no longer strays too far from Rhode Island. In fact, it might just be its new favorite stomping ground.

Black Cats
of New England

Location: Throughout New England
Type of Creature: Feral black cat
Last Seen: Late 1900s
AKA: Black panther

The History

Mr. Hennessey loved nothing more than to share tales of his life with his students. He spun stories of mysteries, family fun, and adventure to help liven his English classes. Whether or not the accounts were totally true was always the subject of conjecture among his 7th grade students. There were certainly many tales that stood out as interesting and unique.

Perhaps the most unusual tale he told his classes was his own personal encounter with a mysterious creature. One day, while roaming the woods outside his New Hampshire cabin, Mr. Hennessey spied something odd in the woods. His eyes quickly darted to a strange creature, as he noticed a veiled black shadow some distance from him. He stopped and watched the four-legged creature walking through the dense woods. Suddenly, he froze… as the creature crossed his path merely hundreds of feet away. It paused a moment, glanced knowingly at him, and then continued along its own personal journey.

Thus, Mr. Hennessey concluded his own personal story of an encounter with a black cat of New England.

While many students chuckled at the story, Mr. Hennessey's tale left many students wondering. Did he really see some strange black cat in the woods? Or was he thrilling them with his own fun, fantasy tale to spice up English class.

Unfortunately, Mr. Hennessey is no longer with us, but the tale lingers as a memory of the phantom cats that have long been associated with much of the United States. Nowhere are these stories more common than the eastern coast, particularly New England.

The Mystery

The stories of the such mysterious black cats have long piqued the curiosity of biologists and cryptozoologists alike. These large cats have been the subject of lore for centuries. The earliest settlers to the region made first notice of these odd cats, sometimes spotting them in the once densely wooded region.

North America is home to only three native "big cats." These include cougars, bobcats, and lynx. None of these animals naturally grow to be black, so the black panthers remain an enigma of sorts. As a way to distinguish them from other native cats and help separate them from large cats that might be mistaken for them, they are often dubbed the "North American Black Panthers" (NABP).

On the TV show *MonsterQuest,* an investigation into sightings of the animal turned up a variety of evidence that suggests people do see these big cats, but there is no conclusive proof that one exists. In their investigation, *MonsterQuest* members investigated photos, skeletal evidence, and videos with no concrete analysis to support the claim that a large black cat roams the countryside of New England or, in recent years, Arizona, Oklahoma, and Texas (where sightings have become more common).

Various theories to explain the NABP have been shared. Most biologists think that people are just witnessing cougars in poor lighting—like at sunset—which may give such cats a black appearance. Other scientists believe the cat sightings are actually misidentified cats that have been seen out of context or viewed without proper perspective.

Black cats have been seen in Massachusetts, New Hampshire, Vermont, and Maine. Perhaps the greatest rash of incidents occurred in Connecticut during the 1950s and '60s. There, during those two decades, countless sightings of a creature were reported throughout the Nutmeg state. Several stories were written in the *Hartford Courant*, describing eyewitness accounts of the cat throughout Barhamstead, Granby, and Simsbury. The creature caused quite a stir throughout the state and sent many people out on chases to determine if, indeed, the cats existed. The sightings diminished during the last half of the twentieth century, but they have occasionally occurred since then.

Exactly what these cats are—or might be—remain unknown, but one thing is for sure…there just might be a strange species of cat roaming New England.

The Black Flash of Provincetown

Location: Provincetown, Massachusetts
Type of Creature: Phantom Human
Last Seen: 1930s
AKA: Phantom of Cape Cod

The History

The 1930s were strange times in America. The country was still embroiled in the Depression and was just a few years away from entering a war in Europe and the Pacific. America was obsessed with movies and radio shows. Sometimes, the more mysterious the show, the better attended it was.

Perhaps it was this sense of mystery that settled over Provincetown in the late 1930s. Or maybe, just maybe, it was something more. For, in 1938, the streets of Provincetown became the home of a mystery all its own.

First, it is important to know a little about the region. Provincetown is located on the tip of Cape Cod. Known for its sandy dunes, tourists spots, and popularity with artists, Provincetown is indeed a creative spot. It was also the original stopping-off point for the Pilgrims when they arrived in America. Soon realizing that the land was uninhabitable, because of the abundant wood, as well as the fact that it housed Native Americans, with whom they fought, the Pilgrims ventured across the bay and arrived in Plymouth.

The Mystery

Provincetown has its own special history, and in 1938, it took a unique turn that might have been forgotten, if not for the likes of several mystery writers of New England. In November of that year, as a woman was walking down the street one cool night, her eyes soon caught the attention of a mysterious black figure nearby.

According to Robert Ellis Cahill, the mysterious creature was entirely black and about eight feet tall. The woman mentioned that it had eyes made of flame and emitted a strange buzzing sound that was like a cicada, or what the locals call a "June bug," only louder. To add to the mystery, the woman said that the creature was dressed all in black and wore a black cape. She didn't stick around for a long look, but noticed it also had silver-like ears.

Perhaps one of the most interesting tales of the Black Flash comes from the newspaper *The Provincetown Advocate*. On October 29, 1939, in an article entitled "Fall Brings out the Black Flash," the newspaper recounts various reports of the unusual creature. According to the article, the creature had been known to scare kids, jump ten-foot hedges, and grab women.

While the newspaper speculated that winter fever might be gripping the region early and that the tales of the Black Flash, though gaining national attention, were pure urban legend, it mentions that an "intensive investigation" of the creature turned up only one person who had spotted it. The man, Captain Phineus Blackstrap, swore under oath that he had seen the Flash one Monday night near an area known as Helltown Road. The captain suggested that the sightings of the creature were common at the time and happened "here every fourth year since I was a man and boy." According to the Captain, the creature never harmed anyone and was believed to have been in actuality not a creature at all, but a lost sailor looking for his vessel near Race Point Beach. Along with this, the captain said he was often seen eating a "skully-joe" (a type of salted cod), which, perhaps, helped entice him to share unusual stories.

The Black Flash sightings eventually dwindled; no one knows exactly what happened to it. However, the story has become a common part of the New England cryptid lexicon and is still referenced from time to time.

The Block Ness Monster

Location: Block Island, Rhode Island
Type of Creature: Sea creature
Last Seen: 1996
AKA: Basking shark or manta ray

The History

Rhode Island is known as the Ocean State for a reason. The state has long been known for its dependence on the ocean. From days of shipping and trading, to an era of mansions, which drew the rich to the coast, to modern-day tourists and yachters, the waters of Rhode Island are an enticement. Many sailors and fishermen alike have made their living off the water, and in modern times, this is no different. Each day, fishermen cast their lot with the ocean, making the daily pilgrimage to the fishing spots off the coast of the country's tiniest state.

Block Island is the largest island located about thirteen miles off the coast of Rhode Island. It is a remnant of the last glacial ice age. Native Americans were first to call the island home, dubbing it Manisses, which translates to "Island of the little god." Dutch explorer Adrian Block visited the island in 1614, giving it the name that sticks to this day. The island has been inhabited since 1661 and is a popular tourist spot.

The Mystery

It was a warm summer day in June 1996. It started like any normal day for Rhode Island fishermen Gary Hall and Jay Pinney, as they left the shores of Block Island, Rhode Island, hoping to catch their share of monk fish that trip. They departed the cozy confines off shore, hoping for a good catch, but little did they know how interesting a catch it would be.

The men cast the nets from their ship, the *Mad Monk*, into the cold waters in a spot called Old Harbor. They knew this place was the perfect spot for a large haul. Indeed they did, as they hauled up the large trough of fish...and something else.

According to accounts of the day, a foul-smelling skeleton came up with the net. The skeleton definitely caught the attention of the men on the ship, and while they were unsure of what the skeleton represented, it did resemble a large snake, about fourteen feet long, with a reptilian head. They looked closer at the skeleton, its sunken eyes, and the strange whiskers on its head, and knew they had made quite a find. The men were certain they had found something unique, so, they hauled the skeleton and fish to shore. There, Hall and Pinney contacted authorities, giving the skeleton to conservationist and fisherman Lee Scott, who preserved it in ice for further investigation.

It did not take long for news of the strange skeleton to spread throughout Rhode Island. Nearly 1,000 people flocked to the island just to catch a glimpse of it. The unusual species gained the nickname "The Block Ness Monster" (for Block Island) and cryptid enthusiasts everywhere wondered if a new species had been found.

Upon further study, the skeleton had ninety-six vertebrae to match its foul smell. The remains were shipped to the National Marine Fisheries Laboratory in nearby Narragansett (on the mainland). There, studies on the skeleton proved inconclusive. While most scientists at the laboratory speculated the remains were of a basking shark, frequently confused for sea serpents, not everyone was convinced. Some speculated that the creature may have been the remains of a manta ray, while Scott actually thought that if it were a shark, then it had to be a new species. He noticed that the laboratory measured the snout of the creature as a foot-long, while most basking sharks had a snout six inches or less.

To deepen the mystery, there were some people who thought the remains should never have left the island to begin with. As a result, someone—or some group—kidnapped the skeleton and made off with its remains. Its whereabouts became a mystery, only deepening the idea that perhaps there was more to the Block Ness Monster than met the eye.

Jay Pinney believed so. He spent time studying basking sharks and trying to identify what creature he and Hall may have caught. He never believed with any degree of certainly that the remains belonged to a shark. From the pictures he saw of the remains of basking sharks, the two creatures did not look alike.

The story of the Block Ness Monster seemed to vanish for good, once the remains were "lost." However, in June 2004, the remains of a similar skeleton was reported off the island again. According to the *Block Island Times*, two men, Rob Fell and Callum Crawford, were spear-fishing off the coast of the island on June 24th, when they encountered the unusual skeleton of something coiled up below the surface. They brought the remains to the surface and unfurled it, revealing an eighteen-foot creature of some sort.

The following day, researchers descended on the island to investigate. They began to study and compare it to other sea life that had washed up on shore. While no one was too certain as to what the skeleton might be, oceanographer, professor, and examiner Jeremy Collie believed the creature was, indeed, very large. Other than that, no conclusion could be drawn.

What is this Block Ness Monster? It is anyone's guess, though one thing is for sure: there seems to be some type of large creature lurking off Block Island. Perhaps it is nothing more than a basking shark that has passed away over time. No matter the source, the Block Ness Monster is indeed alive and well in the minds of those who believe.

Cassie,
the Casco Bay
Sea Serpent

Location: Casco, Maine
Type of Creature: Sea serpent
Last Seen: 1960s

The History

Casco Bay, Maine is an inlet, created by the Atlantic Ocean, jutting into southwestern Maine. As with many of the water forms of the region, Casco Bay serves as the backdrop to a variety of small islands. It is a popular tourist attraction, with visitors flocking to the nearby islands to enjoy the flora, fauna, and waterways.

The Mystery

Casco Bay is also home to one of the most mysterious creatures of the Pine Tree State. Affectionately known as "Cassie," the Casco Bay Sea Serpent is part of the lore that has supposedly stalked the bay for centuries.

The first reports of Cassie date back to the mid-eighteenth century. In 1751, a serpent was spotted in nearby Broad Bay, raising the thought that a sea creature roamed the coast of Maine. In 1779, the first alleged report of a Casco Bay creature was reported when a young ensign named Edward Preble had an eerie encounter with the beast. Preble, a fresh naval recruit, was stationed on a ship called *The Protector*. While patrolling the waters of Casco Bay one day, Preble noticed a strange serpent from his position of the ship.

Preble and the crew watched it for many minutes. The creature even caught the attention of the ship's captain. The captain decided he wanted to learn more, so he did whatever any fearless captain of the day would do—he sent his young ensign out to investigate. And that is just what Preble did. Entering a small rowboat, Preble was lowered into the water to learn more about the odd beast.

Preble approached with caution. As he got near, the creature grew a bit more alarmed. Its long neck rose nearly ten feet from the water. Preble watched as the head of the serpent turned toward him, looked, and then moved away. To prevent a sudden change in plans, Preble fired a round into the air to ensure that the serpent stayed away. It did…for a time.

The following year, a similar "thing" was spotted in Broad Bay. In May, Captain George Little spotted what he believed was a forty-five-foot creature not far from his ship. The head seemed to rise about five feet from the water into the air and appeared to be about the size of a man's head.

According to the Maine Mysteries website, the serpent was again spotted by a variety of people in 1818. It appeared to make a two-month tour of the region in June and July—and then it disappeared for a while.

The next reported big sighting occurred in the twentieth century. In 1912, the Cassie reappeared near Wood's Island, Maine. While traveling on a steamship going from New York to Portland, nearly two-dozen people, including a woman known as Mrs. F.W. Saunderson, watched the creature's neck emerge from the surrounding water near the island. Its neck seemed to rise more than six yards into the air and it remained that way for thirty seconds. The serpent glanced over at the gawking travelers, who were still surprised to see it, and then moved on.

A later, more in-depth encounter was related by a man named Ole Mikkelsen. A Scandinavian transplant to the region, Mikkelson had lived in Maine since 1923. According to Roxie Zwicker, in the book *Haunted Portland, From Pirates to Ghost Brides*, Mikkelson's encounter with the beast occurred one warm June day in 1958. Mikkelson and a friend woke early that morning hoping to enjoy a day of fishing not far from the Portland Lightship, but he came back with a whopper of a tale instead.

While relaxing near Cape Elizabeth, Mikkelson spotted a strange shape not far from his ship. The shape was large and floating near the surface. Mikkelson passed by for a closer look, thinking the shape was actually a submarine near the surface. However, he and his close friend were in for the surprise of their lives. As they got closer to the sub, they realized it was not a sub at all—it was alive and appeared to be some type of serpent.

The men watched as the creature rose near the surface. Its tail came clear of the water and raised into the air as it dove below the surface. The creature then paused a moment, tilting its head toward the men, before moving off toward the Portland Lightship.

According to Mikkelson, the serpent appeared nearly 100 feet long. It swam in the depths of the bay before moving off forty-five minutes later. The creature appeared to have light brown skin with a tail like that of a mackerel. While it was difficult to determine its eyes or sense of sound, it did seem to listen to the call of a foghorn in the distance.

Reports of the serpent have diminished considerably since the early 1960s. While skeptics claim this is simply because the creature does not exist, cryptozoologists are not convinced. An increase in traffic has driven other sea creatures, such as dolphins, from the cozy depths of the bay, so there is little reason to doubt that the local noise may have sent Cassie on its way, too.

Champ:
The Monster of
Lake Champlain

Location: Lake Champlain,
Vermont, and New York
Type of Creature: Sea creature
Last Seen: 2009
AKA: Lake Champlain Monster

The History

Lake Champlain is a body of water found in the northwestern section of Vermont. Helping to form a border between New York and the Green Mountain State, the lake has been a dominant landmark over the years.

Native Americans used the lake during the pre-colonial era. Historians believed that the first hunter and gatherer tribes may have moved into the region about 11,000 years ago. At that time, the lake was much larger and is often referred to as the Champlain Sea. The earliest tribes were likely the first to explore the lake and travel on it.

In the 1600s, Samuel de Champlain, a French explorer, embarked on many expeditions to Canada and New England. During one such expedition, he explored the lake, wondering if it was a path to a larger body of water, or perhaps even the legendary Northwest Passage to the Pacific Ocean. He made an early map of the lake and named it for himself.

Champlain eventually went on to explore the region other times. He did consider establishing a colony in what is now New England, but moved further to the North, settling in what is now Canada. However, the body of water remained named for the Father of New France. It became an important site in the development of the Northeastern Kingdom of Vermont and a major landmark of New England.

Through the years, the land surrounding the lake has been well developed. The lake eventually suffered from this development, becoming polluted. In a strange twist of fate, the lake was designated the sixth Great Lake in 1998. The purpose of this was to gain funding to help clean the lake and restore it to its original beauty. The designation lasted only three weeks. Nevertheless, Lake Champlain has remained an integral part of the fabric of New England and, to this day, it is also home to one of New England's greatest mysteries.

The Mystery

Loch Ness has the Loch Ness Monster, and that is, perhaps, the most famous sea creature in the world. However, second on that list of intriguing sea monsters is none other than the creature that supposedly called Lake Champlain home: Champ. Although no one has ever proven the existence of a monster in Lake Champlain, countless accounts of one have been reported since, at least, the early 1600s, causing many to speculate that there is "something" in that lake.

The first people to witness Champ were the Native Americans in the region. In fact, the Iroquois had a legend about a horned sea serpent that inhabited the body of water. Other Native American groups believed the lake was home to at least one monster that inhabited one of the lake's islands.

According to legend, it was a massive creature, larger than a ship, that often took on the form of a woman and would devour people who passed near it.

Still other Native American groups believed the lake was home to a large, green dragon. According to Robert Ellis Cahill, in the book *New England's Marvelous Monsters*, the creature would often appear on the surface of the lake at night, hoping to eat members of local tribes canoeing under the moonlight.

The first documented account of Champ was from none other than Samuel de Champlain himself—and is more than 400 years old. In 1609, Champlain spent a great amount of time exploring the lake and mapping it. During his exploration, he encountered several Native American tribes in the region. He took note of their tales of the lake.

One story that particularly intrigued him was the tale of the lake's monster. Champlain found it so interesting, like much of the local lore, that he wrote it in his journal. Although Champlain probably did not witness the massive creature himself—many who have read his journal interpreted that he had—he stated that the creature used to eat humans whole. It also had a storage pocket on its body that was big enough to store a ship and was used to house humans that the creature had collected for later eating. It was known to let birds rest on its head and then snap them up with a beak.

Champlain knew that some of these stories appeared farfetched and later qualified the statements:

> What makes *me* believe what they say is the fact that all of the natives, in general, feared it, and told such strange things about it that, if I were to record all they say, Champ would be regarded as myth.

Champlain may not have seen the immense creature of local lore, but he did witness a rather unusual serpent-type creature in the lake. While he hardly described it as a behemoth from the depths, he did describe it more like a modern-day garfish, which is known to call the lake home.

The first detailed encounter with Champ dates back to the late 1800s. In 1873, the *New York Times* printed a story about a crew of railroad workers laying rails on the New York side of the lake. While laying track, the men were interrupted by a strange sound coming from the water. They paused from their work long enough to see a large serpent creature emerging from the water. The men, in fear, took off from the worksite, and soon after, the serpent turned and swam off. In their parting glimpse, the men noticed that the creature appeared to be gray and covered with scales. It also had a small, round, yet flat, head with a hood on it.

The railroad crew sighting was but the first of the creature that year. A steamship carrying passengers on a scenic tour of the lake got more than it bargained for when the ship literally ran into the serpent. The ship lurched and nearly capsized after the collision. Surprised, the tourists and crew looked into the water to see the creature surface near the ship after the collision and then disappear.

During the remaining nineteenth century, many other reports of "creature sightings" brought attention—and tourists—to the lake. In 1883, a local sheriff reported seeing a twenty-five- to thirty-five-foot snake-like creature floating in the lake. Four years later, a local boy reported that his attention was diverted to the lake when he heard a strange sound, much like a steamboat. He was surprised to see that the noise did not come from any ship, but from a peculiar creature in the lake. Another report from that year placed it near the shore of Charlotte, Vermont.

In the late 1800s, passengers on a steamship in the lake also reported seeing the serpent. Reports of the possibility of a Lake Champlain creature grew rampant and spread throughout the country. The reports became so captivating that the great entertainer (and renown audience provocateur) P.T. Barnum was said to have offered $50,000 for its remains.

During the early twentieth century, reports of Champ dwindled. However, by 1960, reports of the serpent began to resurface, much like the creature itself. In that year, on May 20th, a man named Harold Patch stopped by the western side of the lake. There, he sat to enjoy a picnic by the shore when he had the surprise of his life—a giant, snake-like creature emerged from the water, just off shore. Patch studied it for nearly a half-hour as it frolicked on the water. According to Patch, it had a definite snake-like appearance with three, perhaps even four, humps, and was at least twenty feet long.

Walter Hard, an editor who once worked for *Vermont Life* magazine, also spotted it. He saw the serpent one day while vacationing near the lake in 1962. Hard had extensive knowledge of the beast, even tracking a series of stories for his magazine. Still, he had never seen the creature himself until Labor Day of that year. He and his wife were visiting Appletree Point on the Vermont side of the lake, when they heard an unusual noise. They gazed out and noticed a strange head emerge from the depths of the lake. The head appeared as a whitish sphere, similar to a person swimming in the lake. It surfaced for a moment, and then moved along.

According to Robert Cahill Ellis, the creature has been spotted numerous times since the 1960s. During one incident, scuba divers, Morris Lucia and Fred Shanafelt, encountered it while searching the lake for a lost vehicle that had plunged below the depths. While in the water, they saw a sudden movement from behind them. A large head came from the depths to look at them. The creature steered close to the men, its gray body visible and its head stretched out about eight feet from the lake. It tilted its head at them, as if eyeing them with a curious nature, and then moved onto its regular business. The men, Ellis mentions, raced out of the water and vowed never to swim there again.

In 1983 and 1984, visitors to Hero's Island spotted the creature many times and described it in many fashions. At least one person commented that it had three humps coming up from the water, about five feet apart, as it traveled near boats. In July 1984, about twenty-five people spotted the creature swimming near the island as well.

The Proof of the Creature?

Reports of the serpent are not enough to substantiate its existence. Since pre-colonial days, the inhabitants of the lake have reported seeing something, well, fishy, in the lake, but most reports are inconclusive.

However, perhaps the most interesting piece of Champ evidence comes from a photograph taken by Sandra Mansi. In 1977, Sandra and her husband, Anthony, were spending a day visiting relatives near the Canadian border. While driving, the couple stopped by the lake to pass some time. The Mansi children spent time near the water playing, while Sandra and Anthony sat back and enjoyed the afternoon.

Suddenly, while Anthony returned to the car, Sandra saw a strange commotion in the water. The lake began to churn, and before she knew it, a shadowy figure appeared from the depths. The noise caught the attention of her children as well. At first, Sandra and the children were unsure of what it was, but the shadow slowly took the form of a serpent's head and moved from side to side. At length, it appeared to rise eight feet from the water.

The commotion from the water caused Anthony to quickly return. Stunned by the sight, he pulled his family from the water's edge. Together, they sat a safe distance from the water, watching the creature for several minutes, before it moved away from shore. Sandra was able to snap a quick photo just as the creature submerged.

The snapshot, though grainy, helps provide a glimpse at what many people consider to be the main features of the creature. [At the time of printing, this snapshot could be found at the following two websites: http://www.cryptomundo.com/bigfoot-report/champ-photo/ and http://scienceblogs.com/tetrapodzoology/2008/06/03/mansi-champ-photo/.] Although no one report necessarily corroborates another, there are some features that witnesses claim to have seen that are similar in all cases. First, Champ is thought to grow up to forty feet long. It is said to have a horse- or dinosaur-shaped head and a snake-like body. Two horns are believed to protrude from its head. Its skin is often reported to be a grayish color, though some reports suggest it might be a slight shade of rust. The creature is often thought to have humps that move in unison as it moves. Most often, it is characterized as having three of these undulating humps.

While no one is too sure what to make of the creature, there is precedence for the theory of a large lake monster. Dr. Anton Bruun of the University of Copenhagen discovered an unusual species of eel larva while studying the Sargasso Sea years ago. The young eels measured six feet in length and one could theorize that such a creature might grow to immense proportions. Based on calculations, Bruun's eel larva alone could have grown to be 90 feet in length. Further proof comes from a similar creature caught in Japanese nets in 1977. The thirty-two-foot-long creature resembled an extinct plesiosaur that used to roam prehistoric oceans.

Some scientists are quick to point out the lake provides a possible home for such creatures. The unusual length and depth of the lake, which make it much larger than the famous Loch Ness, provide many potential hide-outs. Likewise, the lake, along with its feeding source, the St. Lawrence River, was once a portion of a large sea, and ancient prehistoric life forms have been found in the region. It is possible that a prehistoric species may have been cut off from the sea years ago.

This all begs one question. If the creature does exist, then there must be more than one "Champ" helping to produce future generations. If that is the case, then why has no one ever seen the remains of one? A logical question, indeed. However, it appears science may also have an answer for that. The average temperature throughout the lake, especially at its depths, is 40°F. Such coldness helps to add weight to the remains of any sea life that may die. Along with this, the pressure of the lake has often kept remains from washing ashore. Legend has it that the lake has never offered up its dead—a testament to this unusual pressure. Likewise, the lake itself is more than 400 feet deep in some parts, which could prevent any entity from being seen. It appears, then, the naysayers can't say that a lack of remains disproves the existence of Champ.

Protected Creature

If laws help to prove the existence of crime, then perhaps they also help to prove the existence of this allusive creature. There are laws that actually help protect Champ from bodily harm. In Port Henry, New York, it is against the law to harm or even "harass" the lake monster. In 1981, the serpent—if it does live in the lake—was declared an endangered species and is now offered protections designated as such.

Is there a creature roaming Lake Champlain? Many witnesses seem to think so, a law suggests there might be, and even scientists believe one could exist. However, despite all of these beliefs, no one has ever proven that Champ does exist, though it is more proof that New England is home to some truly remarkable, curious creatures.

What a Champ?

As mentioned, no one knows for sure if Champ is real or not. However, there have been a variety of sightings over the years. Here is a brief timeline of the famous sightings:

1609: Samuel de Champlain writes about Native American reports of the creature.

1819: Settlers near Port Henry, on the New York side of the lake, witness the creature and report being startled by its emergence.

1883: Railroad workers report seeing the creature; a sheriff named N.H. Mooney also reports seeing it.

1887: Series of sightings of the lake creature were reported.

1960: Harold Patch reports seeing Champ while picnicking with his wife near the western shore of the lake.

1962: Walter Hard, former editor of *Vermont Life* magazine, spots the creature while vacationing with his wife near Appletree Point, on the Vermont side of the lake.

1964: Witnesses at the Westport Summer Camp (for kids) report seeing the creature surface on the New York side of the lake.

1973: Several people on a boat witnessed Champ and gave chase, to no avail. The sighting occurred near the Port Henry region of the lake.

1975: A deputy sheriff named Janet Taylor reported seeing a dark creature in the water with its head sticking at least three feet into the air.

1977: Famous Mansi photograph is taken by Mansi family on trip to the lake.

1981: More than a dozen reports of the creature occurred.

2007: Scott Joy, riding on a ferry, reports a sighting of Champ while crossing the lake.

2009: Eric Olsen, a Burlington resident, shoots video-taped footage of the lake that shows a creature in the lake (though, some people claim it is a moose).

Chicken Eating Fish of Stratford Light

Location: Stratford Light House, Stratford, Connecticut
Type of Creature: Fish
Last Seen: 1909
AKA: Chicken eating fish

The History

Connecticut has long held a tradition linked to the sea. The home of fishermen and whalers alike, Connecticut earned a reputation for its hearty sailors and seafaring ways. This has brought much prosperity to regions of the state, including the Mystic seaport. It has also given rise to a variety of fishy stories, including this one.

The Mystery

Perhaps the most unusual mystery connected to the Connecticut seashore is a strange tale that dates to July 28, 1909. On that date, Theodore Judson, resident sailor and lightkeeper (from 1880 to 1921) for the Strafford Light, encountered a most curious creature.

It was not ships and storms that proved the most challenging for Judson. On many nights, he had been awakened to a sound that he said was a cross between a saddened soul and a howling dog. Though an in-depth search never identified a source of the noise, Judson noticed that his pet chickens would mysteriously disappear the day following such strange noises. After several incidents, Judson deduced that the sound must be coming from a creature that had claimed his fowl—and, according to sources, it was quite a haul. More than 200 (some sources say 300) of his beloved birds had been spirited away by this mysterious thing.

However, that July summer night, the mystery would deepen. That night, the sound resurfaced. As all good lightkeepers would act, Judson rushed to the noise, lantern in one hand and gun in the other, perhaps expecting the worst. Arriving on the coast, he surely was caught by the surprise. There, heaving itself on the shore, was a strange creature stirring in the sand.

As he watched carefully, it grew closer and closer. Soon, Judson realized it was a fish. According to the lightkeeper, it was rather flat like a skate, about three feet long, and weighed sixty pounds. It had a mouth that extended its entire head with long teeth similar to that of a shark. The creature was a dark color, likely black, and hard to see in the nighttime sky. The fish continued to scurry onto the shore, seizing Judson's chickens. Judson rushed in, fired the gun, and caught a better glimpse of the creature. It had fiery eyes, the size of a human's, and spines trailed along its back. The thing also had unusual flippers on its underside, like that of a turtle.

The odd fish remained on shore for a few moments before retreating back to the sea. Thus, it became the first noted sea creature to feast on chicken. The strange fish was never spotted again. The story itself remains somewhat of a mystery, particularly since many fish in the area would be hard-pressed to eat a chicken. Whatever it was, there is no doubt that there might be a fowl-eating fish located somewhere in Connecticut.

It should be noted that Judson's creature may seem odd, but Judson was no stranger to odd stories. According to legend, he also claimed to have seen, and temporarily caught, a mermaid not far from the light. Judson had only regretted that had not had enough time to save the mermaid and claim the legendary reward that P. T. Barnum had long offered for anyone who had been able to give him a live mer-creature. Judson did follow-up by stating he had seen between twelve and fifteen mermaids in his lifetime. He even suggested that he had salvaged an oyster-shelled mirror that belonged to one of the mermaids.

Fishy tale? Or something fishy? It seems the world may never know.

Connecticut's Phantom Dog

Location: West Peak region of Connecticut
Type of Creature: Mysterious black dog
Last Seen: 2000s
AKA: Black Dog of Connecticut

The History

The day was clear with a warm wind blowing from the south. Without warning, a strange creature arrives from the woods. It comes closer and appears to be as harmless as a lost dog…but not so fast—it might actually be the supernatural Black Dog of Connecticut.

West Peak in Connecticut is the site of many an untold tale. The hill is the third of what is described in *Weird New England* as the Hanging Hills of the Constitution State. The region is the home of craggy hills, dense forests, and a variety of legendary creatures.

The region also is home to a place called the Gripen Mire, a swamp-like boggy region amid the former volcanic fields of the western section of the state. Although volcanoes have long since been extinct in Connecticut, their remnants remain, as well as the strange tale of an unusual dog of the area.

The Mystery

Sit Arthur Conan Doyle had the "Hound of the Baskervilles." The literary pooch holds nothing to the legendary dog that roams the West Peak section of the state. According to local lore, the dog can be a symbol of good luck or the harbinger of doom, depending on who sees him.

Stories of the unusual dog date back for more than a century. Although no one knows whom this phantom canine belonged too, at first glance, nothing about the dog seems particularly ominous. The dog resembles a regular, earthly pet. It has short black hair, with gentle, sometimes sorrowful eyes, and a genuine need for companionship. The only tip that this creature might not be an actual pup is the fact that it apparently does not leave any footprints behind.

Even the staunchest dog loather would have a hard time turning this optimistic pooch down. However, if legend serves correct, it is best to avoid all contact with the critter. While the dog seems to bring good luck to a person who sees it once, its charm quickly ends. A second sighting usually ends in sorrow for the onlooker, and a third sighting apparently has a lethal ending.

No one knows exactly where the story comes from. However, the best-known purveyor of this tale is a man who may have been the victim of it. According to legend, a geologist named W.H.C. Pynchon first claimed to have encountered the dog. Pynchon spoke of the canine while traveling to West Peak to observe the region's rocks and minerals. While riding on a small buggy, he happened upon the creature not far from the mountain. It seemed affable—and in the mood for human companionship. Pynchon thought nothing of the dog as it followed him down the road a bit.

The dog watched as Pynchon made an in-depth study of the rocks. He kept a safe distance from the man, keeping a careful eye on him. When the man was done, he rode further down the road in the buggy, with the dog following close behind. Pynchon stopped along the road for a brief lunch. The dog waited outside for Pynchon and then followed the man on his return trip to a local inn.

Pynchon enjoyed the company of the stray dog, but noticed something funny. When returning to West Peak, the dog disappeared as soon as they arrived near the site of their first meeting. Pynchon likely believed that the dog returned to its home and likewise did the same.

Pynchon thought little about the dog after that, except for an occasional passing curiosity. Years later, on a frosty winter morning, he returned to the spot of the original encounter with a fellow geologist to again study the rock formations. While traveling to the site, Pynchon mentioned his chance encounter with the dog. As luck—or fate—would have it, the man had also had a similar encounter with a similar dog in the same region.

Coincidence? Maybe.

In the time that passed between their first encounters with the dog, both men heard other locals talk about the canine. They claimed the dog was possibly a ghost or a phantom. They had also heard a local legend that suggested that encountering the dog a second time was bad luck. However, they thought little of the supposed warning.

Just as they were wandering into the area, the two men saw a strange shadow on a rock formation above. There it was—the dog—resting on a nearby rock…as if it had been waiting for them for years. It couldn't be! At least, that is probably what they thought. Far from being a superstitious lot, though, the men didn't give the dog's appearance a second thought… that's when tragedy struck.

Pynchon heard a rumble and the sound of collapsing rock. He turned just in time to see his colleague slip. Pynchon tried to grab the man, but he was too late. A moment later, he was shocked to see the man plummeting from the rocky outcrop and falling downhill—to his death,

A victim of the dog's curse? Perhaps!

According to the authors of *Weird New England*, it may not have been the last sad encounter Pynchon had with the dog. Pynchon returned to the West Peak region once more. Exactly why remains unknown—and exactly what happened there is equally unknown. All that *is* known is that Pynchon never returned again. He, too, died, while traversing the rocky outcrops. A victim of the creature? No one knows...but for those who believe in such a thing, it certainly serves as an interesting warning to stay away from strange black dogs at Connecticut's West Peak.

Since that time, at least six hill hikers are claimed to have met their death at the hands of the dog. Other hikers have died mysteriously in the region of the peak, including one experienced hiker who passed away in 1972. Are these victims of the phantom dog? Again, no one knows for sure....and no one should stick around to find out.

Connecticut's River Sea Monster

Location: Connecticut River in New England
Type of Creature: Sea serpent
Last Seen: 1960s

The History

The Connecticut River has long played a prominent role in the development of New England. The largest river in New England, it has been used to transport items and goods throughout the region. Lumberjacks in New Hampshire often conducted yearly log drives down the river—which proved to be dangerous, so eventually these were discontinued. The river also borders the large towns of Springfield, Massachusetts, and Hartford, Connecticut, where large mills and factories once dominated the land.

The Mystery

The river has also been home to a long-running mystery that has lasted for centuries. According to wayfarers who have traveled the river, it is the home of numerous sea serpents. Most sightings have occurred on the Connecticut State stretch of the river and the part of the ocean that it empties into.

The first recorded sightings of a serpent occurred in the late 1800s, with a man named Mr. Kelley making the first report. While sailing aboard a ship in September of 1878, he noticed a strange creature off the bow of the ship. As he watched carefully, he saw a large head emerge from the ocean water, near the Connecticut shore. The monstrous head stayed above water for but a moment, before submerging back into the water. Although Kelley did not get a good look at it, he saw enough to deduct that its body was about the girth of a large house, that it had a round, hump-shaped back, and that a team of oxen could have easily passed under it had it been removed from the water.

In 1886, the *New York Times* reported sightings that suggested the monster had moved into the river. On September 8th, the residents of Middletown, Connecticut, were all aghast at the sighting of a strange serpent. The first sightings occurred around six in the morning, when two men, Colonel Stocking and Silas Sage, were rowing on a small boat crossing the river. Suddenly, their boat stopped, as if striking a large object, and then, just as quickly, the boat was tossed into the air. Although it did not tip, the boat went airborn before landing in the water again.

Curious, the men regained their composure and began to search for the cause of their near accident. They spotted a large creature nearby moving away from them. A strange noise pierced the early morning light and a giant head rose out of the river. The head itself was described as "the size of a flour barrel with eyes as big as small plates." The head rose ten feet into the air before returning to the rippling waters of the river.

Excited, and perhaps a bit terrified, the men rowed to shore. They paused for a second look and noticed the creature may have been upwards of 100 feet long. They then created a stir of their own, calling any and all who were passing by to have a look at the thing.

Several residents rushed to the shore. At first, it was hard to locate the creature, but then many people spotted it—and reported that it seemed to be moving up river. Exactly where the monster went, no one knows.

The mystery of the Connecticut River Sea Monster still baffles many to this day. Since that time, similar creatures have been spotted sporadically in the region. It has given rise to the notion that perhaps some hidden species of sea monster has called the river home. Some monster enthusiasts believe it may even be connected to—or related to—Champ, found in Vermont. While such claims may seem a bit much, there is no denying that a curious creature might just inhabit the Connecticut River region.

Dover Demon

Location: Dover, Massachusetts
Type of Creature: Humanoid
Last Seen: April 23, 1977
AKA: Aliens

The History

Dover, Massachusetts, is a small town located in the suburbs of Boston. Known for its pastoral settings and large houses, Dover is a fairly quiet place. The town is home to a variety of businessmen, professionals, doctors, and locally famous people. It seems hardly the hotspot for cryptid activity, but in the mid-1970s, it became the site of what is perhaps the most unusual and mysterious New England cryptid of all time: the Dover Demon.

The Mystery

April 21, 1977, seemed like an ordinary day in the quiet town of Dover. Signs of spring were in the air, as the sun set on the town and students got ready for the end-of-school vacation. Yet, before the end of the night, the police station was abuzz with words of a strange creature roaming the streets of Dover.

According to the official reports from the day, the first sighting occurred early in the night. Author Robert Cahill Ellis interviewed the spectators for his book *Things That Go Bump In The Night*. Three teenagers—Bill Bartlett, Mike Mazzocca, and Andie Brodie—were traveling in Bill's car as they turned onto Farm Street...that's when the car headlights caught sight of a strange animal crawling on a nearby stone wall. At first, they thought it was a cat, or perhaps a dog, but then they realized it was a whole lot more. There, before the three stunned teens, rested the strangest thing they had ever seen. It was a creature about four feet tall, its eyes glowing red, and seeming quite attracted to the lights of the car. The head was oversized and watermelon-shaped, and its skin was a light peach color. The creature's oblong head seemed dominated by eyes, with no mouth, nose, or ears to speak of, and its long, spindly fingers appeared to drag across the stone wall. It peered at the teens for a moment...and then disappeared.

When later asked to describe it, the teens felt that the creature looked almost sorry, like a malnourished child.

A couple hours later, Dover teen John Baxter was walking home from a friend's house. Hoping to catch a ride as he roamed Farm Street, where just about everyone seemed to know each other, his eyes caught a figure coming down the street. Certain it was a buddy, John called to his friend... but it was no friend.

According to Baxter, he came face-to-face with the creature along a rock wall. It was about three feet tall, like a monkey. He describe the thing's face as a figure "8" on top of what looked like a baby's body. The thing kept its large, orange eyes focused squarely on Baxter and watched for what the teen thought was ten minutes. Baxter believed the creature was ready to spring at him—and actually feared that it was not entirely safe to be there.

However, the odd being seemed fearful, clinging to its nearby surroundings, and then it turned away quickly and headed to the woods.

The teens all reported what they saw, causing quite a stir in the local towns surrounding Dover. Reports of the creature brought interest from the police, as well as local cryptozoologists. The entity did appear two days later near Springdale Avenue in the center of Dover. That night, it caught the attention of teenagers Bill Taintor and Abby Brabham, as they passed through the town. Again, it seemed quite attracted to the headlights of the car and caused quite a shock. This time, however, the eyes of the creature appeared green.

The teens were all asked to draw the thing they'd seen separately and all three drawings seemed remarkably similar. It appeared the woods were indeed home to something unusual.

Soon after the encounter, Loren Coleman, a foremost cryptozoologist, visited the area, assembling a team of fellow cryptozoologists. He coined the term "Dover Demon" to describe the unusual creature spotted in the woods that night. While some people believed it could be alien in origin, Coleman asked at least one person who was knowledgeable about aliens to investigate the creature. Upon an in-depth investigation, which included Walter Webb, an assistant director at the Hayden Museum located in Boston's Museum of Science, the team concluded that the creature was of unknown origin. Although it seemed far from extraterrestrial—after all, no one reported any unusual activity in the sky that night—it was hard to pin-point exactly what the creature was.

As to the nature of it, many theories have been proposed. Classic UFO believers suggest it was an alien. Some scientists have suggested that it could have been a baby moose. Coleman dismissed this idea, reminding that most of this region of New England was out of the typical moose range (although one adult male has roamed as far as next-door Natick). Cryptzoologist Karl Shuker believed the creature might be associated with a Mannegishi, a creature popular in Cree mythology. Others have suggested it may have been a ghost of some sort. Paranormal investigators have noted that ghosts do seem attracted to teens, and all of the people who reportedly had encounters at the time were teens. There are also those who have suggested that the creature was near an outcropping of rocks that were similar to Pooka stones—fairy homes of rather rambunctious Irish fairies—known as the Pooka Stones.

A couple of things stand out about the case. First, all of the sightings of the creature were in the vicinity of water. There were ponds or rivers near all of the witnessed accounts. Secondly, according to local legend, a man living in Dover claimed to have seen a devil on horseback near the Polka Stones. Along with that, teens in the region told stories about strange occurrences in the woods of Dover.

There are many locals who believe that the legend of the Dover Demon was a prank. Although all the witnesses attest to having seen the creature—and Bartlett even *swore* that he saw it—there are many in and around town who tended to doubt the story. After all, the Demon appeared to disappear shortly after it was seen…and according to some, for a time, there were local sports teams known as the Demons. Coincidence? Maybe. However, Carl Sheridan, chief of police at the time, knew all five kids involved in the mystery and knew all of them to be fairly reliable. The mystery of the creature has puzzled him since. Coleman and his fellow investigators also all agreed that there was no evidence that this was a hoax or prank. In fact, the mystery has brought nothing but questions to those involved in the sightings.

Bartlett has been plagued by the creature since—mostly by those who want to know more, although he did have a strange encounter when something shook his car a year later. He was not too sure if it was the creature, but did not venture out to find out. He happened to see a small figure fleeing from his car and was not sure if it was a prank or not. In 2006, he told the *Boston Globe* that many people seek him out to find out about the creature. Even thirty years later, though willing to share the story, he finds he has become slightly weary. Yet, he still insists that something unusual was on the streets of Dover.

Sherborn resident Mack Sennott later reported that he may have seen a similar creature five years earlier while passing near Dover's Channing

Pond, thus proving that the creature remains one of the biggest cryptid mysteries of New England—and one that seems hard to explain.

More to the Story

While most versions of the story ends here, the following is definitely not *most versions*. There were at least five other people who saw the creature on the night of April 21st and—at the time—did not make much of it. That same night, a family from the neighboring town of Natick happened to be returning from Westwood after spending a quiet Easter dinner at "grandmother's house." As they left Westwood and turned onto Farm Street, nothing seemed that unusual; the family shared tales of their family dinner and day together, but little did they know what would happen next.

As the car wound its way down the twisted, wooded road, the headlights caught site of a stonewall…and that's when it happened.

The light met the eyes of something walking along the road. It stopped, in a panic, and looked up. There, before the stunned family, was the strangest creature they had ever met. It was tan brown—like a hairless cat—with a large face, wide eyes, and no nose. It glanced for but a moment, and then scurried along the brick wall, disappearing over it and into the woods.

After several choruses of "What's that?", the family momentarily thought little of what they'd seen. Perhaps it was a wild creature, or maybe it was someone slightly malnourished. Whatever it was, it definitely was the most unusual thing they had ever seen.

The sighting may have been an afterthought, except for two subsequent events. The next day, news of the original sighting broke in local newspapers. The stories recounted the tales of the teens who had seen the mysterious creature and even printed an illustrated picture of what the creature looked like. Whatever the family had seen was corroborated by others. No doubt there was something unusual in the woods that night.

Perhaps, more interestingly, the encounter with the creature was not all that was unusual about this one particular night. Shortly after the encounter, one family member joked that the thing they'd seen looked like an alien from space. After chuckling at the thought, it became apparent that—

coincidentally—there was a strange set of lights in the sky that night. Not the ordinary airplane-type of lights, but lights that hovered over one spot. The lights then appeared to hover high in the sky over the car…and followed them all the way through the streets of Dover, into the streets of South Natick, through the streets of downtown Natick, and into West Natick, where the family lived, before moving on. The strange lights caused the family to pause and wonder what it was exactly that they saw. Was it more than just a strange animal? There were no regular flight paths that would have caused a plane to take such a trip over the streets of Dover and Natick. It definitely appeared as if something weird was happening in the sky, as well as the ground.

The tale became part of the family's lexicon and is still spoken of today as "the strange encounter of Dover." Little was made of the events shortly after that time—the youngest member of the family was five and the story began to give him nightmares. However, as time passed, and the story was shared again, the family realized they had been a part of one of the most interesting cryptid episodes in New England's history. To this day, they still mention the event, though they've never shared the story beyond family and friends until now.

Their story adds another dimension to the tale of the Dover Demon. Even now, people do not understand what was in Dover that night, but a creature definitely appears to have been present. Crytozoologists and supernatural enthusiasts alike have tried to speculate what the thing was, from strange mutant, to possible alien, to a legendary pukwudgie (see page 107). Since that time, the creature has remained dormant in the Dover woods. Does it still exist? Will it ever be seen again? The answer remains hidden deep in the woods of Dover.

Durham Gorilla

Location: Durham, Maine
Type of Creature: Gorilla or other type of large ape
Last Seen: 1973
AKA: Bigfoot, Osgood the Ape

The History

Durham, Maine, is a docile town located minutes from the coast and the well-known shopping mecca of Freeport, Maine. The town is quiet and tranquil, a step back in time of sorts…which makes it an unusual site for a cryptid encounter. However, that is just what happened many years ago.

The Mystery

The year was 1973, and the summer was a wild one in this small town. During the month of July, something—or someone in an elaborate costume—stalked the cozy hamlet, causing a barrage of confusion for local townsfolk.

The first suggestion that something was amiss occurred early in the month. Four children on bicycles happened to be enjoying a leisurely summer day when, suddenly, they noticed something strange nearby. One of the youngsters, a thirteen-year-old girl, fell off her bike and was soon face-to-face with an odd creature—a monkey or chimp of some sort.

The girl looked at the monkey and the monkey looked back, non-threateningly….then the monkey proceeded to move off into the woods. The children all witnessed the strange creature and then returned to the girl's home to report the sighting. Several days later, the girl's mother, Meota Huntington, saw the monkey too, while returning home from a baseball game. It quickly made eye contact and then raced into a nearby wooded area.

Mrs. Huntington noted that the thing looked large with black hair and, in her estimation, it weighed more than 300 pounds. She mentioned the incident minutes later to people she passed by and several of them took off into the woods, trying to find it. The creature reemerged near Mrs. Huntington's car, watching her from a safe distance before returning to the woods.

Shortly thereafter, an all-out gorilla hunt ensued. About thirty patrol cars scoured the region looking for a mystery ape. A helicopter was called in to search from the sky. Investigators did find some tracks in a nearby cemetery, but believed they had been made by a large bear.

Soon after this incident, other people happened to see more prints in the same cemetery. Investigators were called in and concluded that the prints were made by some sort of creature, but decidedly one that was *not* a bear.

Reports of the "bear" soon diminished after another interesting report surfaced. A local costume shop had rented out a gorilla costume that had not been returned. Coincidence? Perhaps not. Efforts to interview the person who rented the costume failed, as it was revealed that the person had used a false name. Police soon after warned that anyone dressing as a gorilla in the region had better stop…or face consequences.

Perhaps not-so-strangely, the sightings ended thereafter, but stories of the Durham Gorilla outbreak of 1973 are remembered to this day. No one knows for sure if the creature was indeed a gorilla (no one reported an escaped gorilla in the region), a prankster who obviously would have been very overheated in a hot costume, or a hippie (yes, there were some people who theorized that this might actually have been the source of the hype). However, no matter what it was, residents made it a part of the community, dubbing it "Osgood the Ape."

Monster of Glastenbury Mountain

Location: Glastenbury Mountain, Vermont
Type of Creature: Hairy upright creature
Last Seen: 2003
AKA: Bennington Bigfoot

The History

On the surface, Glastenbury Mountain would appear an ordinary mountain in Vermont. One of the Green Mountains in the Appalachian Trail, it would seem like a popular hiking and tourist destination.

However, for those who know the mountain well, they know that it hides a unique and eerie secret. The mountain, which is found in Bennington County, is contained with the borders of the Bennington Triangle, one of the lesser-known geometric regions of paranormal activity. Like the legendary Bermuda Triangle, or the more regionally known Bridgewater Triangle, the Bennington Triangle has been the home of its share of unusual activity over the years.

The Mystery

Glastenbury Mountain was known to the Native Americans of the region long before the first European settlers arrived. Actually called "the cursed land," Native Americans typically strayed far from the area and reserved the land as a home for their dead. They believed the mountaintop was a convergence of the four winds and knew full well to stray far from its summit.

Europeans who arrived in the area had a similar view of the region. They noticed that the air around the mountain held heavy, strange stenches that seemed to envelop the area. The woodlands around the mountain seemed to be dominated by odd, palpable noises that stopped people in their tracks, and the land over the mountains teemed with strange lights in the night sky.

If this was not enough to stop settlers in their tracks, there was another cause for concern. The region near the mountain was a wetland, known for a large swampy area. According to local settlers, the swampland was not a habitat for your typical creature. It was home to some strange, and some believed, supernatural creatures.

Perhaps the most interesting and best-known version of this creature's tale centers around the story of stagecoach passengers who were traveling the rural roads one dark, rainy night in the early 1800s. As the stagecoach wound its way near the mountain, the driver realized that the rain was intensifying and the ground was becoming soaked. The wind and weather were so rough that the horses seemed unusually squeamish. Fearing what might happened if they traveled onward, the driver brought the horses to a halt and decided to wait out the storm.

As the storm wound down, the horses still remained unsteady. The driver and passengers who had stepped outside of the carriage noticed something peculiar in the ground nearby. Footprints! And not any ordinary footprints. Gargantuan ones. The ones not typically found in those parts.

Perhaps sensing something was amiss, they decided to depart…but they were too late. Moments later, the reason why the horses remained wary was clear. A large Sasquatch-type creature came from the woodlands and spied the carriage. Perhaps threatened by the presence of people or the vehicle itself, it launched an attack, pummeling the coach with a few blows and knocking it over. Shocked, the passengers stared at the shadowy being, managing only to see that it had intense eyes and that it resembled a hairy human, before it ran off into the woods.

This is perhaps the first recorded incident with the Monster of Glastenbury Mountain. Better known as the Bennington Monster, it has been spotted many times during the past few centuries. In recent years, people driving near the mountain have witnessed a strange creature resembling a large man with fur. No one has stopped to check out the individual or pay it much attention. In fact, most people take off quickly as soon as they see it.

Is there a mysterious creature in Bennington. If so, what is it?

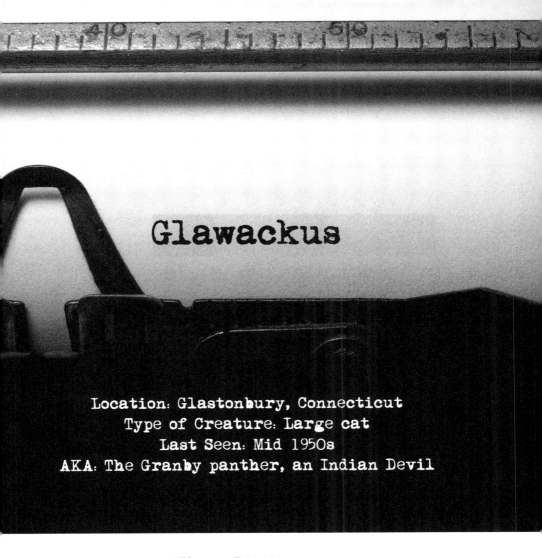

Glawackus

Location: Glastonbury, Connecticut
Type of Creature: Large cat
Last Seen: Mid 1950s
AKA: The Granby panther, an Indian Devil

The History

Glastonbury, Connecticut is a small town located in north central Connecticut. A rather docile town, it is typically the site of idyllic scenes. However, this was not always the case.

The Mystery

The year was 1938 and the town of Glastonbury was under attack. During that winter, animals kept disappearing. Small pets. Farm animals. Other local critters. No animal seemed immune. They would turn up dead days or weeks later. Soon, farmers, homeowners, and hunters kept a wary eye for the mysterious predator.

Although no one caught a good look at the guilty party, many of the people believed that it resembled a large cat. Strange cries heard in the night helped to secure the idea that this cat was a force to be reckoned with.

By January 1939, it became clear that the town had a problem on its hands. Local townsfolk organized a hunting posse to track the creature. For nearly two months, the hunt proved fruitless, yielding only more fuel to the fire that a strange creature was lurking in the Glastonbury region. Soon, though, people began to encounter the beast from a distance. Eyewitnesses began describing a large cat, a large dog, a small bear...and so the creature "morphed" into a trio all its own. Nicknamed the Glawackus (for Glastonbury and Wacky), a new cryptid was born. Everyone was on alert.

In February, residents found more proof of the creature. Strange paw prints were spotted just east of Glastonbury and rumors of the Glawackus grew. Reports came in again, and most people believed it was a half-cat, half-dog animal. It was believed to make paw prints the size and shape of a panther's paw. It had dark fur, perhaps brown or black, with a long, bushy tail, and the animal was believed to be four feet long, standing two to two-and-a-half feet tall.

Citizens in the region scoured every nook, every crevice, every cave in search of the elusive carnivore. Perhaps sensing a chase, the Glawackus went into hiding. It was not heard from for many more years (possibly until the coast was clear?).

The people of Glastonbury rested easy for more than a decade...until the mid-1950s, when the Glawackus was seen again. Residents in the region and surrounding towns reported a strange animal crying in the night. The sounds of the creature resembled the sounds of Glawackus, prompting people to wonder if, indeed, the creature, or its offspring (maybe the son of Glawackus), had returned to the area. Soon, it appeared to migrate to Granby, giving rise to the nickname "Granby Panther." However, just as quickly as the stories of the creature started, they again stopped.

No one knows exactly what the beast is, but it appears to be of unknown origin. However, some scientists and naturalists theorize that it might have been a fisher cat. Fisher cats look like a combination of a raccoon and a large, black cat. Males may grow up to twenty pounds and can be fifty inches long. Fisher cats were not prevalent in southern New England at the time of the sightings and could have been easily misidentified as a Glawackus-looking creature. In fact, the strange cry of the Glawackus would indeed be similar to the unique howls of a fisher cat. Other cryptid enthusiasts speculate that the creature may have been a rare cat that had escaped from a private collection, a misidentified creature, or perhaps even a lone eastern Puma that strayed far from its range.

The Glawackus continues its dormancy to this day. However, it does not prevent people from believing that a strange cat creature still roams the woods of Connecticut.

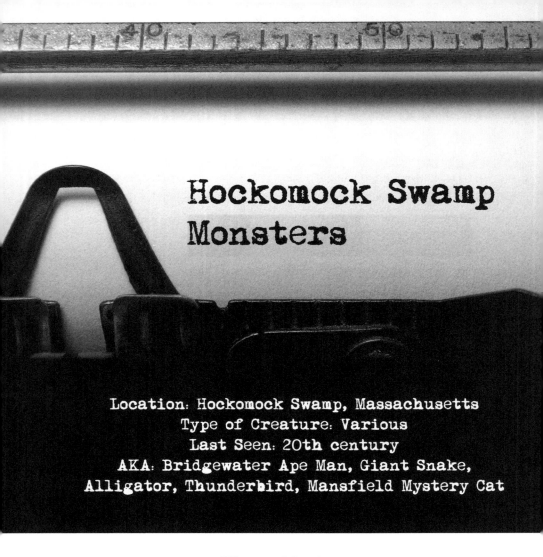

Hockomock Swamp Monsters

Location: Hockomock Swamp, Massachusetts
Type of Creature: Various
Last Seen: 20th century
AKA: Bridgewater Ape Man, Giant Snake, Alligator, Thunderbird, Mansfield Mystery Cat

The History

The Hockomock Swamp stretches through a 6,000-acre wetland in the southeastern part of Massachusetts, reaching into the towns of Easton, Norton, Raynham, Bridgewater, Taunton, and West Bridgewater. The swampy land comprises the second largest wetland in Massachusetts—the largest swamp in the state—and has long been a part of the Bay State's historical landscape.

The name itself is derived from a Native American word meaning "Place where spirits dwell." People have been dwelling in the spot for more than 9,000 years. The region helped lodge deer and moose that early inhabitants to the region thrived on. The swamp was the hideout of Native American Chief Metacom, better known as Phillip, who launched the King Phillip's War against the colonists there. However, settlers knew it by a more sinister nickname, "The Devil's Swamp," for they believed it to be a mysterious and foreboding place.

The Mystery

The swamp is a nexus, of sorts, in the region. Snow melt and rainwater run into the area, making it a dense wetland. Old railroads still stand in the swamp, as do as well-traveled roads, groves of maple and cedar trees, and places filled with sinkholes, muddy rivers, and (supposedly) quicksand.

While the land is considered sacred by many accounts, it is also considered supernatural. It is the home of many strange, unexplained occurrences: phantom lights, large animals, and ghosts have been said to lurk in there. In fact, the region is so well-known for its paranormal activity that noted cryptozoologist Loren Coleman nicknamed it "The Bridgewater Triangle." Paranormal investigators believe that the land, considered holy by the Native Americans, is still permeated by spirits of those upset about the treatment of their ancestors. Local legend has it that the ghost of a Native American can sometimes be seen in the swamp's waterways, often, viewed paddling a canoe.

Perhaps one of the most interesting occurrences in the Bridgewater Triangle involves the tale of a mysterious monster that lurks in the swamp. While a variety of giant creatures purportedly call the swamp home, a large, hairy creature, often compared to Bigfoot, is said to roam the land.

The legend of creatures in the swamp may date way back, but the largest number of reports surfaced in the 1970s. In 1970, in particular, several reports of a strange, hairy biped in the area surfaced. Farmers, whose properties abut the swamp, reported that animals had been attacked, killed, and mutilated by a strange, walking creature. Police checked out the reports, hoping to identify the mystery monster. In one case, an officer on patrol was literally shaken by the sound of his car being lifted in the air by its bumper. He turned around in time to see what looked liked a walking bear heading into a nearby woodland. Police even found odd footprints of a creature that year, but hard evidence of it never surfaced.

During the decade that followed, a variety of witnesses reported seeing a large, hairy creature walking upright through the swamp. Perhaps the most interesting sighting occurred there in 1978. According to the article "Tales From the Swamp" (Ross A. Moscato, *Boston Globe*), a twenty-four-year-old man, Peter Andrade, was wandering through the woods near the Clay Pond section of the swamp in Bridgewater, when he felt a sudden, and unexpected, presence. He turned around in time to see a tall, brown creature walking though the woods. Andrade did not stick around for a closer look.

The article also mentions that five years later, a trapper, Peter Baker, was canoeing in one of the many rivers in the swamp when he heard a loud crashing sound emanating from the woods. He looked up just in time to see a big, hairy creature crashing into the water right in front of him.

Around the same general time, a woman reported seeing a similar cryptid in the swamp, munching on a pumpkin, when she approached. The creature took one look at her and took off into the woods. A report of yet another monster appeared in January 2009, when witnesses abutting the wetlands reported large footprints passing across their land.

Whatever the source, this creature, known as the Bridgewater Ape Man, has caused people from the wetlands area to investigate several times. However, no one has managed to turn up a single sign of Bigfoot or any other of the myriad creatures that supposedly roam there.

However, the Hockomock Swamp Thing is not the only creature that might call this region home. In the 1930s, the Civilian Conservation Corp, created by President Franklin Delano Roosevelt, undertook work in the swamp. While walking through the trails, many of the workers reported encountering giant serpents. These snakes were yards long—about the length of a large vine and the width of a stovepipe. The snakes were never caught and have not been seen since that time, but the nearly eighty-year-old reports are a testimony to the peculiarity of the swamp. According to crytozoologist Loren Coleman, there are some people who believe the snake appears every seven years.

The swamp also has been known to house strange, ghostly lights. While probably not caused by creatures, these ghost lights have been spotted for decades. In the 1960s, at least five witnesses claimed to have spotted them increasing in size and racing right at them.

Native Americans claimed that the mysterious swamp was the home of giant, ancient birds, with wingspans more than ten feet long, called "thunderbirds." In modern times, witnesses have claimed to have seen them and believe that the monstrous birds might be somehow related to pterodactyls. In recent times, many of the birds have been seen from a spot known, appropriately enough, as Bird Hill. In 1984, two of these large birds were reportedly seen fighting in the air over the swamp.

In 1972, the swamp became the alleged home of a strange, lion-like beast. According to reports, residents surrounding the wetlands happened to notice a large cat roaming the area. They also noticed a variety of farm and other animals cut down, with giant claw marks raked across their bodies. A formal lion-hunting party was formed, with members hunting in the swamp and from helicopter, but they turned up nothing.

More than twenty years later, in 1993, a series of sightings occurred again. This time, a strange cat was seen in the vicinity of Mansfield, Massachusetts. Affectionately dubbed the "Mansfield Mystery Cat," people kept a wary eye out for the feline beast. However, as quickly as the cat appeared, it disappeared.

There is no doubt that the Hockomock Swamp region is definitely mysterious. As one person who lived in the region for a long time commented, "There is definitely something unusual about the swamp." It appears the swamp will continue to mystify New Englanders and creature hunters alike in search of many its strange beasts.

Mystic Place or Creepy Destination

The Hockomock Swamp may be home to some unusual creatures, but it is also a downright creepy place for *anyone*. Those who have grown-up in the area know to respect the swampland and many keep a safe distance.

According to legends, here is what you might encounter wandering—or better yet, driving—on the roads that criss-cross the wetlands:

- A Bigfoot-like creature
- Giant snakes
- Pterodactyls or thunderbirds
- Alligators
- Large turtles
- Ghost lights that grow in size
- The ghost of a Native American canoe
- Unusual voices, with no sources, speaking in Native American languages
- Ghosts of colonists
- Quicksand
- A sense of doom or uneasiness
- Compasses suddenly going out of whack

Memphre of Lake Memphremagog

Location: Lake Memphremagog, Vermont
Type of Creature: Sea creature
Last Seen: 1990s
AKA: Memphre

The History

Lake Memphremagog is a large lake that shares the border of Vermont and Canada. Known for its beautiful landscapes surrounded by mountains, the lake is a popular tourist attraction. Summer cottages dot the shore and people go to the lake at different times during the year in pursuit of recreation.

The lake was originally settled by Native Americans. They resided along the shores until the arrival of the first European and American settlers in the early 1800s. The Native Americans welcomed the newcomers to the land, but had an important warning: avoid swimming in Lake Memphremagog at all costs.

The Mystery

Settlers may have been suspicious of the warning at first. Perhaps one might think the original inhabitants were trying to keep the lake free of overfishing or development, but the Native Americans had another reason for sharing such a caution. They believed—in fact, they *knew*—that the lake was inhabited by a strange sea serpent that posed a serious threat.

Whether or not those first settlers heeded the warnings remains unknown; however, the newcomers soon learned for themselves why the lake posed a threat. In 1816, the first recorded account of a creature occurred. Ralph Merry IV, though not an eyewitness, recorded the thoughts and testimony of residents who lived along the lake in a town called Georgeville. According to several residents, a strange creature appeared in the lake. They described a serpent, yet, no definitive description of the creature could be made. Merry theorized that more than one serpent may have inhabited the body of water.

The Merry recordings marked the first of approximately 215 sightings of the Lake Mempremagog sea creature, known affectionately as "Memphre." Many of these accounts have been carefully documented with testimony from actual eyewitnesses. The story of the lake sea serpent took on legendary proportions during the 1800s. However, a variety of fun and lively legends and poems about Memphre were also spun by the characters who lived in the area.

In 1847, several reports appeared in the local *Stanstead Journal*, describing a strange monster that inhabited the region.

In 1961, a fishermen on the lake reported that a large creature, at least twenty feet long, passed by their boat. Frequenters of these waters, the men had no idea what the thing was, but did note that it had a round back and a head that was hard to describe. In the 1990s, several eyewitnesses talked of seeing a three-humped creature in the water. While some claimed it was twenty feet long, others suggested it might be forty to fifty feet in length. One encounter, in 1995, involved two Montreal sailors on film and was used to help support the claim that a creature did exist there.

The potential existence of Memphre has captured the minds of many people in the region. Jacques Boisvert, a diver with a particular interest in the serpent, began investigating reports in 1983. Boisvert founded the International Society of Draconology of Lake Memphremagog to record the many encounters people had with the lake monster. He also created and copyrighted the name of the creature.

Boisvert's hard work added to the knowledge of the cryptid. However, research alone was not enough. Boisvert used his diving skills to personally explore the lake up to 1,000 times. Much to his disappointment, Boisvert never saw the creature, though he did believe that he may have touched it, suggesting that during a dive he thought he once brushed up against a tree stump, until the object swam rapidly off.

No one knows exactly what, if any, cryptid might inhabit the lake. Many cryptozoologists would suggest that the creature—if it exists—would belong in the long-neck family of sea monsters, but not enough evidence exists to verify this as true. Part of the problem in gaining information about the purported monster is that not one definitive description exists to define it. Some people mention that it has the tail of a serpent. Others notice that it has a humped back, while some eyewitnesses suggest that it has a round back. Some have different accounts of its head, while the length of the creature often changes with different viewers, who report that it is between twenty and seventy feet long.

Varying descriptions aside, there are many who believe that Lake Memphremagog is the home of at least one (and possibly more than one) creature. Some believers further suggest that the monster may actually have a larger domain than just that of the lake. Reports of creatures in nearby Bower, Brompton, and Massawippi Lakes resemble the Memphre sightings, suggesting that these lakes might be connected by a series of underground caverns.

In actuality, nobody really knows what mysteries might be lurking in Lake Memphremagog. Yet, every year, an average of eight reports of the creature are recorded with many placing the monster near a point in the lake called Owl Head. Perhaps someday, it will rise to the surface for one and all to finally see.

Mountain Lions of Connecticut

Location: Woods of Connecticut
Type of Creature: Mountain lion
Last Seen: 2000s

The History

For centuries, mountain lions roamed throughout the United States. With the country teeming with wild forests and woods, the environment and habitat was perfect for a large mountain lion population. Over time, people living in the earliest settlements, such as Connecticut, began to clear forests for farmland. Because farmland and mountain lions didn't mix, farmers claimed the remaining woods of the Nutmeg State in the late 1800s. By the turn of the twentieth century, all (or so it is believed) mountain lions were eradicated from the state, migrating to the wild.

The Mystery

Mountain lions have long been banished from the New England region. However, that has not stopped many people from claiming that the large cats have indeed returned. No more is this more prevalent than in the woodlands of Connecticut. There, since the early 2000s, several people have claimed to have spotted the appearance of large, wild tan cats roaming through the woods.

While no scientific evidence exists that the creature has indeed returned to the state, there are many reasons to support why the sightings have increased in the past decade or so. To begin with, there is a greater awareness of species reemerging into suburban areas. The revival of bears, bobcats, coyotes, deer, and wild turkey in New England, and the appearance of such animals in the suburbs, has made people more attuned to the idea that wild creatures are making a comeback throughout the northeast lands. Along with this, people are more likely to report seeing wild animals to authorities. The notion that reemerging species may pose a threat to suburban animals and pets has made animal owners more alert.

Recent sightings of these mountain lions have been linked to Litchfield Hills, Sharon, and Woodbury, Connecticut. It appears that people have seen big cats in these towns, much larger than a bobcat, wandering in the woodlands.

According to the Damned Connecticut website, the Department of Environmental Protection has officially declared that mountain lions do not exist in the state. In fact, several other authorities doubt the reports of such creatures, as well. While the sightings themselves are not doubted, the lack of physical evidence of mountain lions makes it seem highly unlikely that the creature has indeed returned. No paw prints or other such marks have been located belonging to a mountain lion. No dead carcasses have ever been located. And, no photographs have been taken to determine, once and for all, that the big cats do exist here.

However, that being said, there are many people who swear they have seen these wild cats. But, one thing is likely...something big is lurking in the woods of Connecticut...and it isn't your ordinary house cat.

Natick Piranha

Location: Natick, Massachusetts
Type of Creature: Fish
Last Seen: 1990s?
AKA: A released pet

The History

Natick is a large town located just west of Boston. Although a quaint suburb now, the town was originally home to a settlement of "Praying Indians" that bears the town's name. Much of the town developed around this local christianized Native American colony. As more settlers moved into the region, and the King Phillip War decimated much of the original local population, the town evolved into an European colony.

Central to the development of the town was the variety of small lakes and ponds that dotted surrounding landscapes. Many of these waterways provided summer habitation and year-round fish for the locals. Overtime, they became popular bathing holes, boating spots, and ice-fishing homes for the town. In fact, at least one of the ponds, Dug Pond, was the location of a regional ice house.

The Mystery

Natick is called the home of Champions, the home of John Elliot's Praying Indians, and the home of the original baseball (or one used in early baseball games). Yet, it is also the home of a local urban legend.

According to some sources, a lone piranha once called a local waterway its home. While no one seems to know how the piranha got into the lake, a variety of stories were told about its supposed existence. It was suggested that visitors to the waterways, surrounding local Route 135, should be wary of setting foot into the water, lest they encounter the strange biting creature. Some locals believed that a piranha owner released the poor creature into the wilds, no longer willing to care for it. Others suggested—so the legend goes—that it somehow found its way into the water system of Natick.

Was there indeed a piranha in the water? It *is* possible, though no one knows for certain. The urban legend spread during the late 1980s and early 1990s before disappearing.

At any rate, the creature was never officially spotted in the region. Even if it was seen, though, it would have posed little threat. Scientists say that such a creature would never be able to cause injury to large animals or humans on its own. Likewise, many such fish would not be able to survive the long winters in the temperate region of Natick.

North Shore Mastodon

Location: North Shore, Massachusetts
Type of Creature: Mammoth or mastodon
Last Seen: 1950s

The History

During the Ice Age, the terrain around the eastern coast of the United States was much different than it is today. A giant ice sheet covered much of the region, taking large swaths of dirt, granite, and soil from Canada, as it migrated south from the northern areas of the hemisphere.

The Ice Age may have marked a time when the earth's climate cooled; yet, it also marked a time when an amazing assortment of creatures roamed the earth. Species such as sabre tooth tigers, prehistoric horses, and the ever-lovable Mastodon called the icy regions home. While the era of ice ruled the land, these creatures dominated the landscape.

As time progressed and the Ice Age ended, a variety of changes occurred throughout New England. Much of the ice sheet retreated, leaving areas of moraine and kettle lakes in its wake. Along with this, large deposits of granite were left behind (seen as the giant boulders that seem as if they have been lobbed by giants to their current locations). The fading Ice Age cobbled out the remarkable landscape of New England. Cape Cod, Martha's Vineyard, and Nantucket are perhaps the most famous remnant of a time gone by.

The Mystery

These are not the only remnants of the bygone Ice Age, however. As ice melted and oceans grew, much of what was land disappeared beneath the sea. Along with this, the remnants of bygone creatures also vanished beneath the growing tides.

Perhaps the most famous remnant of such a species belongs to a member of the mastodon family. According to scientists, the ice sheet that surrounded New England provided a suitable environment for herds of mastodon. It is very likely that these gigantic elephant-like creatures roamed throughout the land.

In the mid 1900s, one of these remnants came to the surface. Fishermen from Massachusetts went out one day, hoping to make a typical daily catch. Little did they know that their haul would produce a different type of catch. After trawling for fish and bringing the nets to the surface, the fishermen noticed something quite peculiar: a giant tooth was caught in between the fish!

At first, it must have appeared to be the tooth of a giant creature from another era, a mysterious cryptid that once called the land home. Upon closer study, it became evident that this was not the tooth of some unknown creature, but the tusk of a mastodon that had left it behind thousands of years ago.

The tusk helps show the amazing history of New England. It also helps show that, sometimes, evidence of a previously undiscovered species might be little more than evidence of a species that died off centuries ago.

Pigman of Vermont

Location: Northfield, Vermont
Type of Creature: Pig-like human
Last Seen: 1971
AKA: Ghost, pig phantom

The History

Some of the tales you hear about New England tug at the fabric of the landscape. Sea serpents and strange creatures roaming the land are typical fare, but other stories seem quite unbelievable—the heart of the imagination. Such is the case of the Pigman of Vermont. In fact, to hear the story, you would think you were watching a classic horror flick from the 1980s: *Halloween* or *Nightmare on Elm Street...*

But there is something peculiar about this tale. Something quintessential New England. To get the full story, you have to go back many years, when the first tales of the Pigman began to surface, in the early 1950s.

According to urban legend, the story of "The Pigman" may have originated in 1951. Over time, locals told stories about a boy named Sam who was an adventuresome sort. On the eve before Halloween—known as Cabbage Night or Picket's Night in parts of Vermont—the boy decided to grab some eggs and scatter them about town.

As the story goes, Sam never returned that night or the next day. A frantic search for the boy turned up nothing. His spirit disappeared into the mists of the Green Mountains, or so people thought.

Superstitious folk believed a little bit more. Some held fact that Sam's spirit began to mingle with other local animals, forming large human-like pig people that roamed the rural back roads of Vermont.

The Mystery

Now, New Englanders like their yarns…and this one seems to have a lot of twine in it. However, in 1971, it appears the story may have taken a slightly different turn. During that time, in a portion of the Green Mountain State known as Northfield, a series of mysteries began to unfold. First, local dogs started to go missing. Cats, too. Strange noises could be heard at night, and then, according to Joe Citro, author of *Vermont Monsters*, "it" happened.

Locals say that a farmer was roused in the middle of the night by a sound coming from his backyard. Fearful that a large animal might be attacking important livestock—or perhaps assuming that a smaller one, like a raccoon, was getting into his trash—the farmer went to investigate.

Hoping to catch the animal in the act, the farmer decided to turn off the outside porch light. He gazed and looked…waiting for the unsuspecting raccoon, the tiny possum, or perhaps some larger, curious nocturnal creature he expected to find.

His eyes scoured the darkness, until, suddenly, a face came from the depths of night and stared right at him. Face-to-face, outside his window, was the strangest being this side of the *Twilight Zone* (you'll remember the episode). There, he saw it—a most remarkable creature, with cold, dark eyes, long white hair, and a strange pig snout. It stood on all fours and looked at the farmer for a moment, and then it burst off into the darkness.

The farmer swore the creature was the size of a man, somewhere between five and six feet tall. He wondered where it went.

It turns out that the thing was still roaming the landscape. Days later, it returned to the town, perhaps lured by the sounds of a local high school dance. While kids inside were enjoying the festivities, a few gentlemen outside were taking a break from the music. While chatting, and perhaps even sharing a beverage or two, the boys were taken aback by a sudden sound near the school.

They went to check it out and realized they were staring at a most peculiar-looking creature, or man, they had ever seen. They reported it as walking upright, resembling a pig, with bushy, white hair. The boys, terrified, returned to the dance and reported what they had seen, but all that remained of their mystery creature was a few hoof prints in the sand.

Since that time, there have been supposed sightings of a strange, white-haired beast walking upright near the town of Northfield. Is this strange Pigman really a creature, or is someone playing quite a practical joke? No one seems to know, but one thing is certain…if you happen to be driving near Northfield, Vermont, and you see an eerie-looking hitchhiker with white hair and a snout, you just might want to keep on driving.

Plum Island Kraken

Location: Plum Island, Massachusetts
Type of Creature: Kraken
Last Seen: 1980
AKA: Giant squid or Squidly

The History

"Plum Island, Massachusetts, is a wonderful tourist region of the North Shore. It has been cobbled by centuries of wind, ocean, and northeasters. More of a peninsula than a true island, and part of the town of Newburyport, it is a haven for those who love nature. Complete with summer cottages, winter homes, and miles of beaches, the island has long been a hotspot for residents and tourists alike.

Plum Island gets its name from the wild plum plants that grow in the region. It has been the site of many incredible events. Massachusetts's first famous aviator, W. Starling Burgess, established the location as an early source of flight. And Plum Island is home to a national refuge to protect the diverse habitat that calls the island home.

The Mystery

Plum Island has been the subject of several *strange* events during the past centuries. Ships have been known to sink off the craggy coasts, at least one notable Bigfoot encounter has been logged near the national wildlife refuge, and, in the winter of 1980, the region became a focus of monstrous activity, as a legendary and mysterious creature appeared along the shores of the "island."

In February of 1980, one of the "hardest-to-capture" creatures in the world appeared on the shores of Plum Island. There, along the beach, the feared monster that probably gave way to the Kraken legends of old, was spotted gasping its final breaths—a giant squid.

For centuries, giant squids have been an enigma of the marine world. The large creature, known for its epic battles with sperm whales (as evidenced by the suction marks that are often seen scarring the faces of many a sperm whale), is one of the hardest creatures to study. These squids, which roam the ocean depths, have been difficult to photograph in the wild, as well. Hunting them is often a wild goose chase that leads marine biologists and scientists on a dead-end journey.

Little is known about these giants of the sea. However, a variety of sailors and eyewitnesses have reported battling the giant creatures, nearly to the death. The large tentacles of the giant squid offer a formidable foe and can easily snag and drag a human beneath the murky depths of the ocean. The potential dangers of the beast to small ships and other marine craft, eloquently captured in the Disney version of *20,000 Leagues Under the Sea,* could frighten even the heartiest sailor. According to noted folklorist Robert Ellis Cahill, sailors along the Atlantic Coast have had harrowing encounters with the beast, some nearly leading to the death of people on a ship.

In 1980, a member of this lone species appeared on the coasts of Plum Island. Weighing about 450 pounds and measuring about nine feet (with a few tentacles that might have stretched the length to 15 or 16 feet), the squid was perhaps a victim of another sea creature or a powerful storm. It had fought quite a battle, but had lost its two largest tentacles, which stretched up to 20 feet in length. Where the appendages went, or what "took them" still remains unknown. However, the female squid, affectionately known as "Squidly," fought for life on this cold winter day and had enough energy to snap her beak at anyone who ventured near her.

Noticing the creature was obviously a mysterious beast, residents went into action. Experts from the New England Aquarium in Boston were called to the scene. Although they arrived after the creature succumbed to its wounds, they were able to study and preserve it. In giant squid terms, the female was a fairly small creature—some can reach up to twenty to thirty feet in total length (including tentacles). However, such specimens rarely appear on any beach, so the staff of the aquarium quickly recovered it to be studied by experts from the Smithsonian.

No one knows for sure where the giant came from. However, scientists believe that some may breed in the waters off Nova Scotia or Newfoundland and roam the Atlantic waters near the New England coast. While Squidly may be the most famous squid to roam the region, she is certainly not the last one that may call it home.

Pomoola

Location: Northern Maine
Type of Creature: Hairy biped
Last Seen: 1876
AKA: Bigfoot, Indian Devil

The History

In the early 1800s, Maine was a vast, unexplored wilderness. Freshly formed as a state carved from Massachusetts, it became home to a variety of settlers who enjoyed hunting in the wilds of the land. These settlers were the mountain men of Maine, hoping to learn about the wilderness that dominated the state. They explored deep into the heart of the state in an effort to blaze a new frontier.

Hugh Watson was one of these men. A lover of nature and anything wild, he called the region near Mt. Katahdin home. While roaming through the land, he got to know a lot about the wildlife and landscape that dominated it. Large moose and black bears were common in the area, and certainly Watson got to know these creatures like the back of his hand. However, not all creatures were easily explained.

The Mystery

It was on one such journey through the woods that Watson had an incredible encounter with a creature he had never seen before. While walking near his campsite at Telos Lake, Watson felt a sudden, uncomfortable feeling. There was an eerie silence that led to a feeling that he was not alone—a feeling that someone, or *something*, was watching him.

Watson, not fearful of nature, decided to take a look and wandered from his campsite to investigate the woods. Something caught his eye. In the distance, he could see rather unusual, hairy-looking creatures descending upon his campsite. He watched as the invaders began to poke around and check the site, as if looking for something. They remained for quite some time. Fearful, Watson hid that night in the woods, keeping a curious eye on his camp.

The following day, he returned to the site and found it in shambles. The strange creatures had completely ransacked this camp. Watson gathered what was left of his belongings and headed to the nearby town, where locals told him that he was lucky to survive an encounter with these creatures.

Watson's encounter, he soon learned, was connected to the legends of northern Maine that have existed for some time. According to local Native Americans, a half-man, half-beast race of people called the Pomoola (or Pamola) roamed the woodlands of Maine. Legend had it that the creatures were particularly protective of Mt. Katahdin. Some folk even believed that the Pomoola guarded the mountain peak, warding off settlers who might cause it harm.

Watson's story paled in comparison to the tales told by author C.A. Stephens in the 1876 story, "Was it an Indian Devil?" Stephens' story narrates a variety of encounters with the Pomoola, or Indian Devil, of the region. Stephens takes liberty with the text, even speculating that his tales might be a fabrication. However, he provided enough details about encounters to make readers believe that the Pomoola could be real.

Stephens himself claimed to see such a creature while roaming the Maine wilderness. The creatures were hairy beasts that resembled men, and they were not too far from his campsite. Stephens said that "a feeling of sickness or of horror came over me." An ol' time hunter traveling with Stephens suggested that it was safer to stray far from the creature, giving it a wide birth.

Over time, the stories of Watson and Stephens—and others like them—have become part of the fabric of Maine. While no one knows exactly what the source of the Pomoola sightings is, they exist to this day...making one wonder: What exactly lives in the wilds of Maine?

Ponik: Lake Monster of Pohengamook

Location: Lake Pohengamook
on the border of Maine and Canada
Type of Creature: Sea serpent,
plesiosaur, or perhaps a giant sturgeon
Last Seen: 1990s AKA: "The Great Beast"

The History

Lake Pohengamook is officially a Quebec lake located on (or officially one mile from) the border of Maine. The Lake itself inches toward the international border and comes from a Native American term meaning "rest and wintering, sheltered from the north winds." Native Americans dominated the region around the lake until the early 1800s, when a mass exodus of former colonists from America and the Europeans seeking a new life began arriving at border towns such as this one.

The lake is a freshwater lake known for its red-colored water. The tint comes from the large amount of rust that has washed away from nearby mountains. Local divers avoid this lake because of its murky depths, which reach 135 feet.

95

The Mystery

The mysterious depths of the lake have long been a deterrent for those who dared swim in the lake. However, there is something far more interesting that has supposedly called this body of water home for centuries: a lake creature, affectionately known as "Ponik."

The earliest Native American inhabitants here allegedly claimed the lake was the home of a sea serpent. Calling it "The Great Beast," Native Americans warned settlers that the creature patrolled the lake and could be potentially deadly to those who ventured into the water.

The first official report of the serpent dates back to 1873. In that year, a lumberjack named Louis Berube was walking near the lake when he spotted strange fish in the water. According to Berube's report, the fish was large and, in his terms, seemed to be "cavorting" on the water. Not long after Berube's sighting, a man named Benoit Levasseur wandered near the lake. He noticed a large creature, up to thirty feet long, resting on the surface of the water. The beast dove deep, surfaced again, and then took a second plunge before never being seen again.

Since that time, more than 1,000 sightings of the creature have been reported, according to the Crytozoo-oscity website. According to the site, one of the more dramatic sightings occurred in 1944. A young boy was swimming in the lake's water while his father worked at a nearby shore. Suddenly, his peaceful day was shattered by the sound of mashing metal. He quickly looked up to see a strange creature coming toward him, its long tail rubbing against a metal rake that he had brought into the water. It then surfaced near the boy and stared momentarily at him—revealing a face much like that of a horse. The creature then departed and swam away.

While no one has found official evidence of the serpent, many eyewitnesses swear that the creature has been seen swimming the waters of the lake. The sightings have so stressed the people of the region at different times that some have avoided contact with the lake altogether. However, the existence of a creature has not scared *everyone* away. In 1957, a priest named Leopold Plante spent a day on the water, fishing near his church that bordered the lake. While casting his line and reeling it in, he noticed how calm the water appeared. Perhaps, too calm, and then, not far from his boat, a strange shadow crossed the water. A large creature, having what appeared to be two humps, floated in the water. Before he knew it, it was gone.

In the past few decades, sightings of the creature have been on the rise. Much of this activity probably has little to do with the actual serpent and more to do with the fact that a road had been built around the lake. With more people traveling along the water body, there is little doubt why sightings of Ponik have increased.

Ponik is still seen to this day. One of the more unique sightings of the creature happened in 1990, when Guy LeBlanc, the mayor of the town of Pohenagamook, population 3,000, took a day-trip on his boat into the water of the lake. While enjoying the sun and water, LeBlanc noticed a strange ripple appearing close to his boat. He took one look and saw a rather large creature swimming beside his boat.

According to LeBlanc, there were no other boats on the lake at the time. Because of this, LeBlanc knew that some type of serpent was in the water and that it was responsible for the ripples that were being made. While LeBlanc may have initially suggested the idea that a sea creature caused the ripples, he actually believed the beast may have been a big sturgeon. In fact, a number of the supposed sightings have been strangely reminiscent of the description of a large, sturgeon-like fish.

LeBlanc's sighting seemed to unleash an avalanche of similar reports. Several people have come forward since that time, suggesting that the creature continues to surface on the lake. Many of the eyewitnesses suggest that it resembles a horse, or has humps, or flippers. Some of them claim that it walks on nearby lakesides on the shore or resembles a plesiosaur.

LeBlanc and many in the area certainly enjoy the notion that the lake might be host to a strange water creature. Rewards have been posted for evidence of it. Tourists continually visit in large numbers to see Ponik, and the area even has a festival to honor it.

Is there a creature of the lake? No one knows...and no one wants to doubt it.

Provincetown Sea Monster

Location: Provincetown, Massachusetts
Type of Creature: Sea creature
Last Seen: 1719
AKA: The Franklin Sea Monster

The History

Benjamin Franklin is one of the most beloved American patriots of all time. Known for his keen wit, his scientific mind, and his superb writing skills, he was truly a Renaissance man. However, many people do not realize that his uncle, also named Benjamin Franklin, was a major influence in his life. Uncle Ben had his own rapier wit and was known to spin quite a yarn… like the one that follows. According to legend, Franklin supposedly "saw"— and was the main witness of—a creature off the coast of Provincetown, Massachusetts.

The Mystery

Provincetown has long been tied to the ocean. Native Americans fished off the tip of Cape Cod. The Pilgrims first explored the region, hoping to find a suitable place to settle. Whaling ships, fishing ships, and whale-watching boats have all called the town home, but, in 1719, something else may have called Provincetown home, too.

On September 28, 1719, a strange creature made its way into the Provincetown harbor. Sailors who were quite familiar with most types of sea-creatures, where taken aback when a most peculiar-looking sixteen-foot beast rose from the water.

According to reports of the day, the creature was more like a beast from mythology. It was a serpent of sorts, with a lion's head and curly hair and beard. Jutting from its mouth were large teeth that look ready to bite a ship in two. The monster itself had a peculiar yellow color and a short tail as it came up from the water. It broached the surface for moments, causing a sensation on the whale ships nearby.

Moments later, harpoons in tow, whalers descended in their whaleboats and chased after the beast. The fight was on. One harpoon, then another, then another struck its mark. The beast roared out of the water and charged the ships—the ships barely managing to elude the creature. It then took to open water, whale ships in quick pursuit. The harpooners again fired at the beast, missing their mark. The whaleboats continued their pursuit for about five more hours, before giving up the chase and returning home.

The story sounds like pure fiction, and it might be. Reports of sea monsters have permeated the Provincetown shore, but nothing quite this extreme. Most people believe the creature was merely an invention from the mind of a rather clever man: none other than Ben Franklin, the Uncle. Indeed, it could be. The next time you are in Provincetown, though, take a second look—you just might see the sea monster of Provincetown.

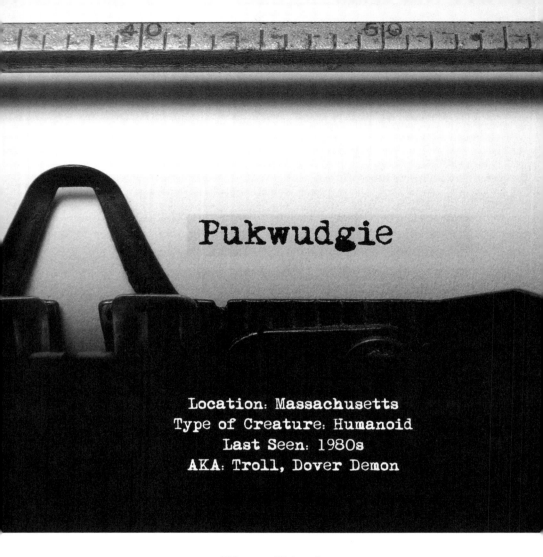

Pukwudgie

Location: Massachusetts
Type of Creature: Humanoid
Last Seen: 1980s
AKA: Troll, Dover Demon

The History

The original inhabitants of Massachusetts, the Wampanoag nation, have been an important part of the fabric of the Bay State for centuries. Perhaps most well-known for being the first people to encounter the Pilgrims in Plymouth, the Wampanoag probably called Massachusetts home for hundreds of years before the Pilgrims arrived.

The Wampanoag developed their own culture in the region. At the time of the arrival of the first European explorers, visitors realized that the Wampanoag were powerful people who had made a large contribution to New England.

The Wampanoag helped the Pilgrims survive their earliest years and have become a part of the unique history of Massachusetts. As part of this history, many legends have been passed down over the years about the land and the places they called home. Perhaps one of the most interesting, and fearsome, is the legend of a unique group of humanoid creatures known as "Pukwudgies."

The Mystery

According to Wampanoag legend, there once lived a giant, named Maushop, who roamed the local countryside. Maushop was a beloved figure of the Wampanoag. The gracious giant helped carve out Cape Cod and earned the pride of the tribe.

The Wampanoag's feelings for Maushop were not shared by a race of little people known as the Pukwudgies. The Pukwudgies were large, troll-like humans, with gray skin and glowing eyes, that stood between two and three feet tall. Whether or not they were true humans or human-like creatures remains a subject of conjecture. However, what is indisputable is the contempt they felt for Maushop.

The Pukwudgies tried hard to befriend the Wampanoag and help them survive life in New England, but most of the time their attempts went awry. As a result, the Pukwudgies decided to go against the Wampnaog, wreaking havoc in their villages and surrounding lands. Their scorn for Maushop and the Wampanoag soon became evident throughout southeastern Massachusetts. The Wampanoag called upon the Maushop to help them, and soon he rounded up as many of the creatures as possible and destroyed them.

Remaining Pukwudgies rallied against the gentle giant and tried to destroy him. According to some legends, he was killed in the waters off Massachusetts, while in others, he simply left the area.

The story of Maushop and the Pukwudgies seems pure legend, but, as with many tales, the legend seems to have taken a life of its own. There are many people who have claimed to see Pukwudgies in the woods and forests of New England to this day.

Legend disputes exactly what the Pukwudgies are, but the Native Americans of the region believed they were best left undisturbed. Pukwudgies were believed to be able to use magic, conjure fire, transform into a porcupine-like creature, and appear and disappear. They also had powerful poison arrows that they shot at unsuspecting victims.

According to the website Pukwudgies: Myth or Monster, these creatures have been spotted in Freetown, Taunton, and Framingham, Massachusetts, as well as a cemetery in New Hampshire. Several of the encounters have been particularly chilling. A woman in Freetown claimed that she had seen a Pukwudgie in the local forest. The grey creature, with a rather large belly, looked at her with its green eyes, long nose, and large lips. Surprise etched on its face, the creature stared until the woman and her dog realized that the best thing to do was leave. The woman claims that the thing still visits her at home from time to time, gazing in her windows. In Taunton, a woman was supposedly scratched by such a creature, and in New Hampshire, similar occurrences have been reported. In Framingham, a man claimed to have seen an orb in the local woods. Following the orb, he encountered a similar small, gray humanoid creature. It came close to him and the man soon took off. Later, the same man recounted seeing such a creature a second time. This time, he was parked, and his car started unexpectedly.

The most startling appearances of the creatures have been connected to Freetown State Forest, a more than 200-acre section of Freetown. Many of the encounters have occurred in that spot and more than one may have had tragic endings. It seems that Pukwudgies could supposedly overpower people and often lure them to their deaths. It is said that the creatures would lead unsuspecting humans to the ledges of a cliff and force them over the side. At a place called "The Ledge" in the forest, a variety of unusual deaths have been tracked over the years. Most of the deaths are attributed to suicides, where people jump off the "Ledge" to the quarry rocks below. However, in many of the cases, the people who had allegedly killed themselves had left no tell-tale signs that they were depressed or had considered killing themselves, leading many to wonder if indeed these creatures might be causing the deaths of people to this day.

Myth or fact, legend or monster, the story of Pukwudgies still fuel the imagination. In fact, some cryptozoologists believe that the famed Dover Demon (more on this on page 57) was a Pukwudgie.

These creatures may or may not exist, but if you happen to be wandering through the woods and encounter a three-foot, gray-looking troll, it might be best to turn and walk (or run) the other way.

The Sea Monster of Gloucester

Location: North Shore, Massachusetts from Gloucester to Nahant
Type of Creature: Sea creature
Last Seen: 1914
AKA: North Shore Sea Monster

The History

Since the time of the first European visitors to North America, the North Shore of Massachusetts has been a staple of nautical culture. By name alone, "the North Shore" shows that a certain degree of the populace subsisted on maritime economy, and, indeed, the North Shore's history is intertwined with the ocean.

Gloucester is well-known as a fishing seaport throughout the country. Fishing boats leave the port daily to cast their lines for the treasured fish that once used to teem off the waters of Massachusetts. Long days, harsh weather, and pounding waves mark the lives of those who lived in the often-idyllic seaside village.

Salem, to another extreme, made its money through the international shipping trade. Once one of the most important port cities in America, Salem garnered fame for its trade with Asia—not its witch trials. Sailors, captains, and merchants alike made money from the famous China Trade that permeated the landscape during the early nineteenth century.

Beverly, an often-forgotten sea town, brought a different maritime fame to the area. Drive through the town and you will be sure to see signs proclaiming that Beverly is "the home to the American navy." Washington's meager force, predominantly privateers, anchored off the Beverly shores during the early days of the American Revolution, protecting the shore lines from British warships that preyed on unsuspecting villagers.

With a rich maritime culture, there is little doubt to the reason why so much ocean-bound folklore thrives in the area. From war heroes, to famous shipwrecks, to tales of ships that went to strange lands, the North Shore has its own rich maritime traditions. However, one of the most interesting folktales involved a series of sightings, which have persisted until modern times, of a strange animal found off the shores of Cape Ann. Tales of this strange sea creature, often called the "Gloucester Sea Monster," have challenged the mind, inspired the imagination, and added to the lush heritage of the North Shore.

The Mystery

The first mention of a sea serpent off the coast of Massachusetts dates back more than three centuries. In 1639, John Josselyn, a visitor to the New England shores, reports a story he heard regarding a sea serpent in Cape Ann. He mentions that the serpent was often seen lying on Cape Ann rocks, but Josselyn got his information secondhand. According to the story he heard, a boat carrying two Native Americans and English fishermen passed near the creature, but when the fishermen suggested shooting the creature, the Native Americans warned that a failed attempt might have fatal consequences.

The most celebrated sighting of the sea serpent occurred in 1817. During that year, it was spotted numerous times in the waters around Gloucester, often passing close to ships in the harbor. The serpent's appearances started simply enough, with a brief sighting on August 6th of that year. Two women and a swimmer were near the water's edge when a strange object appeared in the water. At first, it looked like nothing more than a shadow, but then it became apparent that the object was more like a physical creature.

The first sighting brought little more than a few chuckles and some raised eyebrows, but, by months end, August 6th would prove to be no joke. As the month progressed, more people saw it. The creature swam past ships. It appeared before numerous members of town. Citizens who were well-respected, such as clergy and judges, reported seeing the strange thing in the water. The sightings were met with skepticism in many scientific circles, but flocks of people came to the town in hopes of seeing the strange serpent.

David Humphreys, a respected general and former member of George Washington's staff, was so awed by the reports that he decided to investigate himself. He arrived on the scene and began to gather eyewitness testimony. According to his research, as well as reports in *The Boston Messenger,* a newspaper of the time, the sea serpent ranged from sixty to seventy feet long. It had a head, larger than a dog's, similar in shape to a turtle's. It appeared to have a foot-long horn, similar to a spear, protruding from its head. Its body was equivalent to the width of a barrel and it moved around in snake-like fashion, easily able to turn at a moment's notice.

Although the creature remained elusive, the emergence of such an unusual species caused great excitement in the community. Several fishermen stepped forward to corroborate the initial reports of the cryptid. On August 14th, a shipmaster named Solomon Allen III noted that he had witnessed the serpent for three straight days. The following day, about two dozen people reported seeing the creature playing off shore.

While there were many sightings, a fair amount of the populace doubted that such a creature existed. Despite such doubts, the reports of the serpent persisted for some time. Soon, a $5,000 reward was posted for the creature.

A few hunters ventured in the water in hopes of netting or even shooting the cryptid. However, it was too sly, evading any attempt to stop or capture it.

On August 18, 1817, the scientific organization known as the Linnaean Society of New England began its own investigation of the serpent. Using the efforts of a local man, Lonson Nash, the testimony from eight witnesses was used to gather a composite of the sea monster. Witnesses disagreed on its appearance—some said it was black and others noted it was brown. Some thought the creature looked like buoys while others referred to the body as "cask"-like. Even the length of the creature varied. However, it became apparent that all eight witnesses, who had frequented the water, believed that the creature was something they had never seen before. After gathering information and sorting through the reports, the society decided that an entirely new type of sea life had been discovered, though they still were not certain what it was.

The serpent made various appearances off the shore of Gloucester for the remainder of the year. In September 1817, a sea captain in Rockport, Massachusetts, claimed to have killed a giant snake in the water that stretched nearly three feet long. Some people believe that the snake might have been the progeny of the Gloucester sea serpent. The Linnean Society eventually obtained this snake and studied it, linking it to the Gloucester sea serpent and finally declaring that overwhelming evidence made them conclude that a new genus had been discovered. They quickly dubbed it *Scoliophis Atlanticus* (or Atlantic Humped Snake).

The news was not widely embraced. In fact, many scientists had their doubts about the creature, and when it was later discovered the Linnean Society's specimen was in fact a misshapen terrestrial snake, the doubters of the Gloucester sea serpent came out in full-force. Some people thought the reports were simply a publicity stunt, drummed up to bring visitors to Gloucester. Others believed the publicity of the sea serpent caused more people to think they had seen such a creature as well.

The following summer, the serpent supposedly reemerged off the coast of Maine and Massachusetts. It was spotted in Portland Harbor and near Salem during the months of June and July. In mid-August, it appeared in

Ipswich Bay, prompting a local whaling captain named Richard Rich to track it down. After a two-week search, all that Rich was able to find was a rather large blue fin tuna. Although he declared this to be his monster, many doubt that he actually mistook the tuna for the creature and simply wanted to return with *something*. This made many skeptics wonder if the sea serpent was actually a misidentified creature.

During the summer of 1819, the serpent made the last of its spectacular returns to the area. In June, it was spotted by a schooner passing close to Cape Ann. As the summer progressed, reports of the serpent surfaced throughout Massachusetts, with sightings in Scituate and Boston, among other places. Finally, toward the end of summer, the serpent found the waters near Nahant to its particular liking. Hundreds of people reported sighting the cryptid on the shores off the causeway-linked town. More people rushed to the town to catch a glimpse of the famous monster.

However, as quickly as the serpent arrived, it disappeared. After 1819, the reports of the creature are fewer and far between. In fact, it would appear almost as if the creature had totally left the New England region for, perhaps, better feeding areas, much like migrating whales do during a change in season.

In 1822, the sea serpent emerged again in Nahant. According to reports, it appeared every day during the summer. It took a brief respite from the Massachusetts waters until 1826, when it returned on a similarly daily basis in the waters off the coast. The serpent also made regular visits to the region in 1833, 1834, and 1835.

Author and New England sea serpent researcher J.P. O'Neill advises that reports of the sea serpent were sporadic after the mid 1800s. In the article "The Great New England Sea Serpent," O'Neill mentions that many of the sightings would be forgotten, if not for the work of Gloucester resident George Woodbury, who kept a personal scrapbook of sea serpent sightings. Woodbury's book shows that the sea serpent again appeared in 1844 off the coast of Marblehead, as it suddenly raised its head out of the water, surprising two children who were breaking the Sabbath law with a Sunday sail.

The scrapbook contains other anecdotes as well. Supposedly, the serpent reappeared in 1878, off the coast of Plum Island. There, several children watched a serpent-like creature swim off the shore before it disappeared.

Another gem in Woodbury's scrapbook suggests that a fishing crew ran into the serpent, or another one like it, not too far from the coast of Boston. The crew of the ship *Philomena* found it entangled in the ship's nets. While trying to remove the serpent from the netting, the crew ended up in a fierce, "Jules Vernes esque" battle, as the men tried to tug the net and its load back out to sea. With the help of two other ships, the men were eventually able to subdue and kill the creature, which they said was about sixty feet long and as round as a large tree trunk, with black skin covered in barnacles. The captain of the ship, a man named McKinnon, regrettably cut the serpent loose after the battle, but acknowledged that the monster (affectionately called Big Ben) had been spotted by his and other ships' crews during the previous twenty years.

Woodbury's last account places a similar creature, perhaps a relative of Big Ben, near Cape Ann in 1914. There, each crew member of the British schooner *Flora M* witnessed a snake-like serpent emerge from the depths of Massachusetts Bay. The head resembled that of a horse, as it moved quickly away, disappearing under the ship, and then resurfacing ahead of it before vanishing. Was it possible that yet another creature survived?

Whatever was sighted in the waters off of Massachusetts remains unknown. Yet, to this day, the story of the Gloucester Sea Monster makes people wonder what exactly lives off the coast of the North Shore.

North Shore Sea Serpent Sightings

1639 Cape Ann: John Josselyn hears a tale about a sea serpent that rests on the rocks in Cape Ann. He is told that fishermen and boaters are encouraged not to shoot it, for fear that the creature might attack.

1817 Gloucester: Famous sightings of the creature brings hordes of people to Gloucester, particularly in the summer. The Linnean Society of New England announces that the sea serpent represents a new genus of creature. This new genus is later discovered to be a land snake.

1818 Salem, MA and Portland, ME: A sea serpent is again spotted. Captain Richard Rich (not to be confused with the comic book character) attempts to capture the serpent, but fails.

1819 Nahant: A sea serpent, perhaps related to the Gloucester creature sightings, is spotted. Mobs of people flock to town in hopes of spying the serpent. Large interest in sea serpents is sparked in America.

1822 Nahant: A sea serpent is regularly seen, nearly everyday in the summer.

1826 Massachusetts: The sea serpent reappears off the coast.

1833-1835 Cape Ann: Reports of the sea creature resurface.

1844 Marblehead: Two boys report seeing a serpent's head emerge off the shore.

1876 Plum Island: Children and one adult witness a serpent swimming in the waters off shore.

1912 Massachusetts Bay: Crew members of the *Philomena* and two other ships engage in a fierce battle with what appears to be a serpent-like creature in the ship's net. The creature succumbs to wounds suffered in the battle and is released.

1914 Cape Ann: Crew members of the *Flora M* all report seeing a serpent in the waters off Massachusetts.

Sea Snake of Cape Cod

Location: Coast of Cape Cod,
particularly near Nantucket
Type of Creature: Hybrid sea creature
Last Seen: 1964s
AKA: "The Great Beast"

The History

The waters surrounding Cape Cod have long teemed with creatures that have brought wonder and prosperity to the region. The earliest explorers noted the abundance of codfish in the waters of the peninsula—hence its name—and made a fortune off the fish in the 1600s. In the 1800s, the waters in, around, and eventually far from the Cape Cod area became the hotbed of the whaling trade.

The waters have also been home to a variety of creatures that influenced and perplexed the people of the Cape. Sharks, particularly in modern times, have posed a threat and an interest in recent years. Whales and dolphins have been known to strand themselves on the coasts. Decaying sea creatures have often caused quite a stir on the land, sometimes being mistaken for things other than what they really were and sometimes…there are strange and unique creatures that have been said to lurk in the waters off the Cape.

The Mystery

Perhaps the most interesting creature spotted in the waters off Cape Cod was first seen near Nantucket Island in 1957. That year, the crew aboard the fishing vessel *Noreen* happened to notice a disturbance in the water—and spied an odd creature. The beast looked like a true marine mutt, complete with the head of an alligator and a seal-like body. The six men on the ship watched this creature glide across the water, as if feeding, and then move below into the watery depths. It appeared on the surface at least four times during a twenty-minute period and, according to the men, was at least forty feet long.

Five years later, a similar creature was spotted by a group of deep-sea fishermen off the coast of Cape Cod. They watched as it surfaced, inhaling a lot of water into a barrel-shaped mouth, before disappearing.

In 1964, the *Blue Sea*, a Norwegian fishing vessel, was plying the waters near Nantucket when the three-member crew became awestruck by a strange creature that surfaced near the boat. At first, it appeared to be a whale surfacing for air.

According to Robert Cahill Ellis, in *New England's Marvelous Monsters*, the three men aboard the *Blue Sea* quickly realized this was no ordinary whale. It resembled a hybrid cross of animals. While the head looked like that of an alligator, the body contained humps. At the top of the head was an unmistakable blowhole, and the end of the body displayed what appeared to be a lobster-like tail.

The men watched the strange creature play in the water near their ship. It moved toward the trawler, turned, went northward, and disappeared. The men returned to New Bedford and reported the thing; the Coast Guard and several other boats went searching for the creature. A few days later, a ship called *The Friendship* reported seeing a creature like the one spotted by the crew of the *Noreen*, miles away from the original encounter. The ship circled the creature to investigate and mentioned that it appeared to have barnacles and that it held its tail in a vertical position.

After that, reports of the beast came to a halt. Exactly what the creature was, or might have been, remains lost to the course of history, although, according to Ellis, many scientists theorize that it was indeed a whale shark. The physical makeup and behaviors of a whale shark—large mouth, unusual shaped head, and ability to inhale lots of water—are reminiscent of the creature mentioned in all of these accounts.

Sidehill Gouger

Location: Hill regions of New England
Type of Creature: Badger, wild sheep, wild goat
Last Seen: Modern times
AKA: Sidehill badger, Sidehill Winder

The History

The topography of New England has changed a great deal over the centuries. The once lush, forested areas of the region are now dominated by small towns and villages, with cities sprinkled in for good measure.

Early settlers used to tell tales of how the original landscape of New England once teemed with so many trees that it was possible for squirrels to cross the states without ever once touching the ground. As more and more settlers moved "west," and just beyond New England, they blazed trails throughout the area. These trails, along with the early ones of the

Native Americans, still exist today and look like they have been forged out of the wilderness.

Many a person traveled along these paths. However, according to New England lore, other travelers may have crossed there as well.

The Mystery

The first inhabitants of the region carved entire colonies out of the woods. Cutting trees and using the timber for homes, ships, and industry helped build the northeastern section of the country into a hotbed of migration in the seventeenth century. It also made a distinct impression on the land, as trails were blazed through forests, across rivers, and into the hard, hilly landscape of the interior.

As a result, animals had to adapt to the changes in the environment. Migration took a toll on some, sending them to other places in the country. In some cases, legend tells us that nature took control, creating new creatures out of old ones. It is one such legend that describes the nature of the Sidehill Gouger—a legendary creature that some people claim still inhabits parts of New England.

The Sidehill Gouger is said to have originated in New England and has long been believed to be part of the lore of New England. According to legend, the creatures have been spotted in America since colonial days.

These animals were truly an oddity of nature. A variant of sheep inbred with cows (some say on purpose), the Gouger has disproportionate legs, with those on one side of the body longer than those on the other. This made the gouger perfectly suited for a hillside habitat. Because of their unusual leg structure, they rarely strayed far from their hillside homes. Gougers walked carefully wherever they roamed: one false step meant that a creature might fall into a crevice, or other dangerous spot, and starve to death. They were believed to typically travel clockwise or counter-clockwise based on which set of legs were longer. Some were even believed to grow fur only on one side of the body. Gougers, being herbivores, feasted on plant life found on tops of mountains and hillsides. They often lived in small packs.

Females supposedly gave birth to six to eight pups, which brought stability to the population.

Their existence may have been initiated by their crossing the ocean back during the early migrations to America. In England, people believed that some badgers had different sized legs and acted similarly to gougers.

Gougers go by many other names, such as a sidehill ousel, wampahoofus, and sidewinder, but the common name is "Gouger." The wampahoofus was a version of the gouger thought to live only on Mount Mansfield in Vermont. In Hy H. Tryon's book *Fearsome Critters*, it is said that the Gouger gets its name because it is an animal that used to roam the woodlands that had been gouged by New England lumbermen. Once wild, gougers formed wild pockets that could be found in the hillsides of New England.

Some folklorists believe that small bands of the creatures migrated westward and eventually settled in other regions of America. A large pack of these creatures is said to have once lived in California. Over time, most of the gougers in New England died off and the species was believed to have become extinct in the area.

While there is little evidence to support the existence of the gouger, many people throughout New England have claimed to see these strange animals while roaming the hillsides of New England. Sidehill gougers have been spotted in the western hills of Massachusetts, as well as the mountains of Vermont and Maine, so, perhaps, there is a long-lost species of animal located throughout New England just waiting to be discovered again.

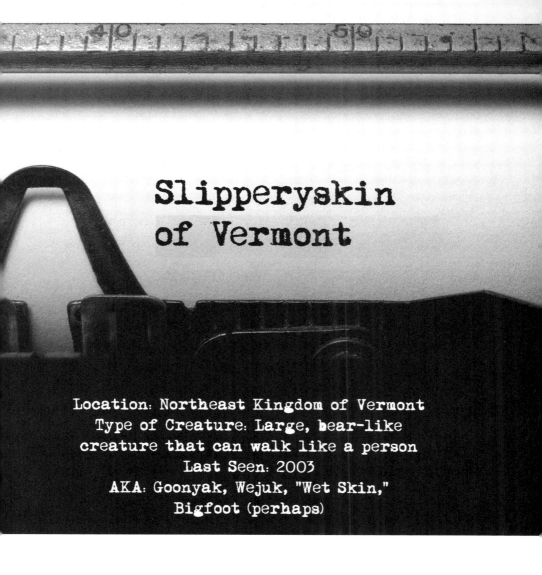

Slipperyskin of Vermont

Location: Northeast Kingdom of Vermont
Type of Creature: Large, bear-like
creature that can walk like a person
Last Seen: 2003
AKA: Goonyak, Wejuk, "Wet Skin,"
Bigfoot (perhaps)

The History

The Northeast Kingdom of Vermont is the picturesque northeastern corner of the state. Known for its scenic vistas, rolling mountains, and beautiful forests that glow like fire in the fall, this corner of the state is a popular tourist attraction.

The term "Northeast Kingdom" was first used to describe the section in 1949. In that year, U.S. Senator George Aiken (who also served as Governor of the Green Mountain State) dubbed the region with the popular moniker in a speech.

The area was home to Abenaki Native Americans during the pre-colonial era and several early settlers called the Northeast Kingdom home during the colonial period. Shortly after the Revolutionary War, settlers began arriving in larger numbers. There, they encountered many woodland creatures, among them moose and black bears…and perhaps something else

The Mystery

According to legend, the Northeast Kingdom is the site of one of the strangest creature encounters in Vermont history.

In the late 1700s, as more houses and towns became established in the region, a strange phenomenon began to occur. People would wake up from a hard night's sleep and notice that their gardens were disheveled. Or their fences were uprooted. Or their cornfields had been vandalized. Or their livestock had been scattered. Or maple syrup buckets would be filled with pebbles and stones.

At first, the occurrences probably seemed more like common pranks. Surely, some ambitious bloke or even some ill-behaved child was at play. However, as their regularity persisted, it became clear that someone—or something—else was clearly at work. After all, who would be causing such frequent turmoil throughout the land. Worse, whatever the source of the disturbances, it seemed to hide its tracks quite well.

The mystery began to unravel when the actual source of the disruption began appearing. Children were the first to see and describe it: a strange creature that looked like an odd mix of bear and human. It had a long coat of fur, with a bear-like face, yet could walk upright on its hind legs. The beast certainly scared children throughout the region.

As soon as the thing was described, people realized that it looked startlingly like another creature that had been spotted in the area. According to author Scott Wheeler on the website Vermonter.com, a strange creature had been spotted by "Duluth," a member of Roger's Rangers, in 1759. The scout had been returning from a raiding party fighting the Odanak Native Americans during the French and Indian War. Duluth wrote in a journal that he kept that, during the return from Mempremegog Bay (ironically, a location of another curious creature), the British and colonial soldiers had been bothered by a "large black bear, who would (rain down) large pinecones and nuts upon us from trees and ledges." Duluth also mentions that the local Native Americans knew of this creature and called him Wejuk or Wet Skin.

Soon, adults began to notice it often, too. Marion M. Daley, in *History of Lemington, Vermont*, mentioned that the creature became well-seen throughout the land and, because it seemed to elude every trap set for it, it earned the nickname "Ol' Slipperyskin." Kingdomers began to view it as a type of bear, and the hunt was on. Yet, this bear had clever ways of eluding any hunter it ran into.

One of the search parties took men to an area of Vermont known as Morgan. Rifles in toe, the men scoured the logging region, looking for the creature, but Ol' Slippersykin was onto them. As they were passing nearby Elon Mountain, the silence of the hunt was soon disrupted by a loud sound. The men scattered, sure that the beast would be bounding down the hill and easily nabbed. Instead, they saw a giant stump roll past their hiding places. No doubt Ol' Slipperyskin was in no mood for trespassers. Having the good sense not to attack the creature that day, the men returned home.

A second search took the men to the area of Lake Willoughby (a site of yet another curious creature; see page 139). There, a group of clergymen had gathered for a picnic. Enjoying the day, they were disrupted by a giant bear that charged into their party. The men scattered in all directions while the bear, looking remarkably like Ol' Slipperskin, "pulled a Yogi" and took their picnic treats. The men truly headed for the hills and most of them regrouped later, safely. However, one man was missing. After a long search, the party concluded the man had been eaten by the creature, as remains were found of what was thought to be a human. However, upon later investigation, the remains turned out to be a strudel. Yes…a strudel. The missing man was eventually found alive and well, though tired, in nearby western Massachusetts, having attempted to run from the creature.

Around 1815, Jonas Galusha, the governor of Vermont, decided to take matters into his own hands. He vowed to rid the state of Ol' Slipperyskin once and for all. Toting a rifle on his arm, he took a part of hunters and headed for the Northeast Kingdom, to a town called Maidstone, where the thing had been recently seen destroying piles of hay and stealing ham from a smokehouse.

Having a reputation as a stoic hunter and having served valiantly during the Battle of Bennington, in 1777, Galusha invented a new strategy to catch the old creature. Now exactly what happened next is somewhat of a mystery—and true Yankee legend if there ever was one. Local lore has it that Galusha took out a jar of strange ointment he had brought for the occasion and covered himself in the scent of a female bear. After rubbing it on quite well, he charged into the woods alone, certain he would find Ol Slipperyskin (or perhaps an amorous male bear or two).

Indeed, he encountered some type of beast. Whether or not it was the true Slipperyskin remains part of legend. However, the story suggests that he came running out of the woods with the creature in hot pursuit. Exactly which creature followed him may remain subject to conjecture: was it Ol Slipperyskin or a flotilla of male bears? Galusha raced to a nearby campsite, startling hunters who were also looking for the creature, with Ol' Slipperyskin right behind him. The creature charged in and took off, the stunned hunters never even managing a shot at the cryptic beast. The creature managed to disappear, as did Galusha's poll ratings. He had already served as sixth and eighth governor of the state, but was not re-elected to the post again.

While stories of Ol' Slipperyskin began to diminish after 1815, the old creature may have left a legacy. According to Joseph Citro's blog, the creature's descendents may still be roaming through Vermont. Occasional sightings of such a beast have still been reported throughout the state. In the fall of 2003, a man named Ray Dufresne had an encounter with a remarkably similar creature while dropping his daughter off at Southern Vermont College in Bennington. According to Dufresne, he was driving by the site of nearby Glastonbury Mountain (yet another site of a curious creature; see page 66) when his eyes caught a glimpse of a strange beast near Route 7. Dufresne describes it as looking like a person in an ape costume. While Dufresne initially thought it had to be a practical joke, he knew that many of the people in the area were hunters and no jokester would dare try to pull a joke like that in such a place. The creature had similar features to Ol' Slipperskin, including long arms and hair all over its body. Shortly after the incident, other people claimed they had seen a similar monster.

Many cryptozoologists believe Ol' Slipperskin is simply another name for Bigfoot. Other historians believe that the early encounters may have been a Native American or another regional settler in disguise, unhappy at the influx of immigrants to the region. The mystery of Ol' Slipperyskin may never be known, but there is no shortage of mystery surrounding this uniquely unusual creature.

Springheel Jack

Location: Worldwide, Massachusetts
Type of Creature: Large biped,
half-animal, half-man
Last Seen: 1940s
AKA: Black Flash

The History

Since the days of mythology, half-human, half-animal beings have baffled our imaginations. Scores of people during the age of ancient Greece, Rome, and Egypt believed in centaurs, fauns, and other unusual creature-humans. It staggers the imagination, and some people believe such a creature once roamed New England.

The Mystery

One such creature has mesmerized the people of New England since the early 1800s. This one is none other than the seldom-discussed, but sometimes seen, Springheel Jack. According to legend, Jack is half-human, half-beast and has been found throughout he United States. Eyewitnesses suggest he is a tall, thin man, who is half-human and half—you got it—animal. He dresses in a long, thin cape, has large claws, and eyes that burn (or glow) a bright red. Jack gets his name because of his capability to jump quite high into the sky.

The original reports of Springheel Jack surfaced in the 1830s. In 1837, he was tracked to the house of a woman who supposedly heard a knock at the door and, upon opening it, with candle in hand, she spotted Jack up-close. Angered, he spewed a blue-white flame at her and began to attack, until the woman's sister came screaming down the stairs. Officials were unable to track this man-beast, and he got away.

Since that time, he has been spotted in other parts of the United States. In 1877, he was tracked and shot at, but managed to escape, unharmed, as bullets flew through him. In the 1930s, Jack got around, being spotted in London, New Mexico, and Cape Cod, Massachusetts. Many of the Cape Cod reports occurred between 1935 and 1943. Instead of spewing flames, he was known to belch at them. According to one eyewitness in Provincetown, Springheel Jack startled a local dog. Its owner, angered, charged at Jack, but Jack merely laughed and bounded over an eight-foot fence to get away. Because of his unusual gait and mysterious appearance, some people connect his appearance to that of the famous Black Flash of Provincetown in the 1930s (see page 28) and believe they are one in the same.

Sightings of the strange man-beast still occur to this day. He is known for a pungent odor that emanates around him. The most recent sighting of this creature occurred in England in 2005. There, people reported seeing what looked like a half-cat, half-man creature resembling Springheel Jack.

Thunderbirds of New England

Location: New England
Type of Creature: Large bird
Last Seen: 1500s
AKA: Pterodactyl

The History

A large bird soars high, looking over its dominion. Its wingspan is four times bigger than the height of a person. It scours the ground, looking for prey. A deer. A buffalo. Perhaps, or maybe it is looking for something—or someone—else. A quick burst of wind lifts it into the air and out of sight. In its wake, a rush of clouds fill the air; moments later, the clouds burst open. Torrents of rain, wind, and thunder erupt across the sky.

Sound familiar? If so, then perhaps you've heard of the thunderbird, the legendary flying creature that permeates various Native American myths from the plains, southwest, northwest, and northeast.

While the legend of the thunderbird may span a variety of cultures, the stories of these birds remain remarkably consistent with many of the stories having similar elements. Almost all point to an incredibly large bird (some almost say pterodactyl-like) soaring…with thunder commencing right after it leaves, believed to have been precipitated by the enormous wingspan. The bird also had powerful supernatural powers, which made it an important element for some cultural ceremonies. Many of these cultures have legends associated with the thunderbird, and people have often wondered if they really did exist.

The Mystery

The legend of the thunderbird is no stranger to New England. The Passamaquoddy Native Americans of Maine had one of the best-known beliefs about the birds. According to their legends, thunderbirds were benevolent creatures that kept a safe watch over people of their region.

While some people viewed the thunderbird as a protector, other Native American tribes viewed the creature with terror. Many of the Algonquin tribes knew it as a bird that dominated the sky. It was the size of a human, with a wingspan nearly twenty feet wide. Its head seemed proportionally smaller to its body. According to reports, the creature would swoop down from the sky as part of its hunting process. Although it did not typically hunt humans, some Native Americans believed that it was responsible for the deaths of unwary people. The creature was such a figure of fright in the air that the simple sight of it would send many of the Algonquin into hiding.

Little is known about the creature, and with good reason. If it did exist, most people did not stick around to learn more about it. As colonists entered the region and the land of the Native Americans dwindled, stories of the thunderbird dissipated. According to the Strange New England website, the last mention of a thunderbird in the area occurred in the 1500s in Pennacook, New Hampshire.

Exactly what the creature is—and where it may have gone—are as much a legend now as the creature itself. However, even in present times, there are people throughout New England who claim to have spotted large birds in the sky…claims that hearken back to a time and place when thunderbirds ruled the air.

The Turner Creature

Location: Turner, Maine
Type of Creature: Land quadruped, like a dog
Last Seen: 2006
AKA: Feral dog, Maine Mutant

The History

The area near Turner, Maine, is a pristine spot, known for its scenic views and off-the-path vistas. Located near the foothills of western Maine, it is a small town with its own charm. Tourists have often come to the spot for a visit and the region itself is known for its quiet atmosphere.

The Mystery

The ambiance of the region began to change slightly in the early 1990s, when a series of unusual events began to occur. Residents of Turner, Litchfield, Lewiston, Greene, and Auburn, as well as other towns, became home to an unusual creature stalking their neighborhoods.

The first encounters occurred around 1991 when residents began hearing piercing cries in the night. The cries were not the typical howls of cats or dogs—or even the coyote—but of an evidently unearthly beast that roamed the night.

Shortly after the weird cries were heard, eyewitnesses throughout the area began spotting an unknown creature wandering the land. According to reports, the creature was about the size of a large dog. Many of the eyewitnesses believed it had glowing eyes and a disarming odor. Several residents, who have had their fair share of encounters with wild creatures, reported encountering the beast and mentioned it looked like nothing they had ever seen before.

The creature reportedly roamed here until 2006. It wreaked havoc on local animals and was blamed for attacking many pets that had returned home injured or were found dead. The first eyewitness account of the animal attacking pets occurred in nearby Wales, Maine, in 2004. There, a man noticed a strange beast emerge from the woods and charge at his Doberman Pinscher. The dog was mauled in the attack. The rash of strange reports caused animal control officers to patrol the towns and, in the process, one officer actually saw the creature. Although he was unable to catch it, he described it as looking much like a wild hyena. During November 2005, the mutant-like animal reportedly attacked a Collie-Shepherd-mix dog. At the time, no one was too sure what attacked the dog, but it was believed to be a large creature capable of inflicting damage.

For months, the identity of the thing and its actual existence was speculative at best. Residents theorized that it might actually be a lynx or bobcat, but that all changed in August of 2006. In that month, a strange creature was found near Route 4 in Turner, Maine. It had been struck dashing across the road, in front of a car, while chasing a cat. The creature was struck and killed. It resembled the animal that many eyewitnesses claimed to have seen roaming the county.

It was the size of a large dog, about fifty pounds, with hair that had an unusual blue tint. The creature had a long snout, almost ratlike, and a bushy tail—unlike any type of animal commonly found in the region. While pictures were taken, it was hard to identify it. Photos did not turn up any likely matches, and by the time authorities could arrive at the scene, much of the body had been scavenged. However, an unpleasant aroma did surround the creature.

According to an *Associated Press* story from the time, Maine cryptozoologist Loren Colen investigated the creature. He, like many of the scientists who studied it, was not totally convinced that it was all that strange. Coleman was fairly certain the creature was not a domesticated animal, but probably a feral dog of some sort. It may have even been a dog that may have been a house pet at one point. While most of the animal remains had been scavenged, Coleman did find a claw that suggested the creature belonged to the Akita dog breed family. Coleman, perhaps the world's leading cryptozoologist, believed that the creature did not evolve from some mystery species, but suggested that it was remarkably similar to an animal found in northern Maine years before the Turner creature was found. Stories of such things have persisted for years throughout Maine and many stories about mysterious dogs abound in the woods of the region.

Exactly what the Turner creature was remains unknown to this day. However, it is evident that some strange beast roamed the Maine woods in the 1990s.

Ware Swamp Monster

Location: Ware, Massachusetts
Type of Creature: Alligator
Last Seen: 1922

The History

Ware, Massachusetts is a small town located in the central, western section of the Bay State. Known as the home of the Swift and Ware River, Ware has been a cozy hamlet for centuries. First settled in the early 1700s, the town grew to prominence as one of New England's cotton cities until the Depression hit the area hard.

The Mystery

Ware is also home to one of the more unusual creature incidents in Massachusetts history. In late spring of 1922, a rash of large lizard sightings were reported in the part of town known as Dismal Swamp. The first reports appeared in the *Boston Globe* on June 6, when Stephen Faerykewicz, driving a Gilbertville Bakery truck, noticed a strange-looking creature near the swamp while making deliveries. He initially thought it was a giant log... until it moved. Trying to prod the six-foot beast along, it growled at him. He knew that it was best to let the beast alone, but reported it upon returning to town.

Shortly after, James Toomey, a veteran of the First World War and hunter, heard about Faerykewicz's encounter. He went in search of the mysterious creature. Believing it was a turtle, he took to the swamp with rifle in hand. Sure enough, he spotted it diving beneath the surface before he could shoot it. Toomey was fairly certain it was an alligator, having spent enough time watching it to recognize the snout and eyes.

No one is too sure what it actually was; most people who spotted it and initially thought it was a lizard speculated that it was an alligator. While alligators are by no means foreign to New England, they are typically relegated to the region's zoos. People theorized that the potential 'gator may have been a pet that had grown too big or, perhaps, it was a reptile that had escaped from a traveling show or circus.

The appearance of a possible alligator in the region definitely captured the hearts and minds of residents, though. Several more people went to the swamp on would-be alligator hunts, swearing that they would bring 'em back alive. Locals went so far as to nickname the alligator "Socrates"— though exactly why remains unclear.

On July 3, 1922, it appeared that the mystery of the alligator had been resolved. According to a *New York Times* article on Independence Day, residents of the town were amazed when Bernard, George, and Leo Satz displayed a four-foot alligator they said they had caught on Gilbertville

Road, near the swamp. According to the captors, they managed to lure the alligator out of its home by shining their automobile lights into the swamp, coaxing the would-be mystery creature out.

While diehard creature hunters may have been disheartened that the mystery animal had been finally caught, residents of the town breathed a sigh of relief…that is, until a reporter went sniffing for a good story—or at least a good picture—and found out the mystery alligator had a story of its own. It had arrived by train the day before from Florida and was planted in the swamp...a true New England hoax, if there ever was one.

Over time, reports of the Dismal Swamp creature, alligator, or giant lizard subsisted. To this day, no one is too sure what may live in the swamp, if anything. Perhaps there is a giant swamp lizard calling Ware home…just waiting to be found.

Werewolf of Dogtown Common

Location: Glocester, Massachusetts
Type of Creature: Werewolf
Last Seen: 1984
AKA: Crane Beach Creature

The History

Dogtown Common is a legendary section of Gloucester. Once the home of a colonial settlement in the town, the area has a history all its own.

The Common was originally a portion of Gloucester established away from the coastal regions of town. The settlement provided a shelter of sorts, in the late 1600s and early 1700s, from enemy French ships, as well as pirate vessels that sometimes scoured the shores of New England, preying on small, coastal villages. For a period of time, the settlement was a fairly prosperous place.

Following the end of the Revolutionary War, the need for a settlement so far from the sea waned and people moved out. As more and more people abandoned the area for the more coastal sections of Gloucester, the settlement evolved into a ghost town. A stout group of citizens remained behind, but time and nature eventually took their course, as these hearty citizens soon passed away.

In the wake, the remains of the settlement turned into a state of disrepair by the early 1800s. A few widows lingered in the houses that had been long a part of their families. Many of these women lived with large dogs that helped protect the house—and them—from wayward strangers who happened by the settlement and often squatted on the land.

Eventually, the last of these widows passed away and a various characters took up residence in the decaying remains of the houses. These characters included two women who described themselves as witches and whose own unique kind of magic brought a variety of visitors to their doorsteps. Another resident, named Daffy Archer, was known for her own brand of medicine: making special brews from the mucus of snails. Archer became a local superstar of sorts, known for a wolf-toothed necklace that adorned her neck.

Many of the residents were wanderers who settled into the common for short periods of time before moving onto other towns.

In time, the last of the residents died off and Dogtown was the home of once-domestic dogs that roamed the streets and woods of Gloucester. These dogs helped give the town its nickname and have helped to add to the mystery of the town.

In time, residents of Gloucester paid homage to the town in their own way. A sailor turned self-proclaimed fighter James Merry decided to hold his own brand of wrestling on the site. In 1892, he put on a public bout pitting man against beast, vowing he could take down a bull with his bare hands in the old Dogtown Common. He successfully took down the beast. For some strange reason, though, he returned on the night of September 10, 1892, alone, in the dark, to hold a private rematch with the bull. In the end, no one is quite certain what happened, but James Merry was found dead with his throat ripped out.

133

Dogtown might have drifted off to obscurity had it not been for a local resident named Roger Babson. A noted economist, businessman, and founder of Basbon College, Babson was also a philanthropist. He loved his hometown and took it upon himself to excavate the old Dogtown section of town. Many of the early foundations of the colonial homes were uncovered. During the Great Depression, Babson hired Public Works employees to carve words of inspiration on boulders. These boulders evolved into a philosophical park to those who visited the area. They remain to this day.

The Mystery

Dogtown has long been a mysterious section of town. Local legends suggest that it may be haunted. People who have visited the site have reported strange sounds, unusual orbs, and the presence of people who might have once lived there.

However, in 1984, Dogtown was also the site of something far more unique. According to a few reports, Dogtown served as the temporary home of an unusual dog-like animal that may have resembled a wolf. In the spring of that year, a strange creature was spotted near Crane's Beach in Ipswich. Identified as a rather large and hairy dog, people passing through the area happened to see it on a dune overlooking the beach. The mysterious dog seemed to disappear when anyone noticed it.

A few days later, a similar creature was spotted in Dogtown, as eyewitnesses walking through that part of Gloucester happened to see a large dog. Others heard strange, piercing howls crying through the night. Exactly what the creature was remains unknown, but many connected the creature of Ipswich to the one located in Dogtown.

To this day, no one knows the species of animal found at Dogtown. Over time, though, people have speculated that this creature might be a North Shore werewolf. Such a wild leap sounds like pure folly; however, according to the New England folklore website, there are a few reasons that such a connection has been made.

First, the town itself was nicknamed for the packs of wild dogs that roamed through the streets. Folklorist Robert Cahill Ellis, in the book *Things that Go Bump in the Night,* mentioned that some Native American tribes in the area believed it was possible for a human to transform into part-man, part-wolf by eating a local herb. This legend, along with the fact that Daffy Archer was known to wear a wolf's tooth and that James Merry may have been attacked by a mysterious creature—and not a bull—have made some people wonder if a wolf-like animal might have inhabited the area for decades. The connections were made stronger with the more contemporary events of 1984.

Time has passed, and since then, and there have been no further reports of strange, wolf-like creatures in Dogtown. However, there are some who express little reservation that werewolves might indeed be found in the North Shore.

White Moose of Maine

Location: Woods throughout Maine
Type of Creature: Large moose
with white coloring
Last Seen: 2002
AKA: Albino Moose, Ghost Moose,
Giant Moose, Spectre Moose

The History

Majestic. Regal. Downright dangerous…particularly if you get too close. These words best describe Maine's most unique and powerful woodland creature: the moose. Moose are large animals that populate the Pine Tree State. Occasionally, these wayward wanderers migrate close to the main streets and backgrounds of Maine, and can certainly scare a wary driver.

Moose practice the fine art of stealth and can find food quite well in the woods. They are large animals found in many woodland and swamp regions of Maine, often standing about seven to eight feet tall and weighing up to 1,500 pounds. They can wander throughout New England (and some have traveled to the suburbs of Massachusetts), but typically, they shy away from well-traveled paths. Encounters with the creatures can be dangerous because they have been known to charge humans.

The Mystery

Ahab had the white whale. The woods of the Carolinas and Virginia have a mysterious white deer. The hunters of Maine have the white moose or, more correctly, the Spectre Moose.

The Spectre Moose is a legend that has existed at least since the early 1900s and sources indicate that the story likely dates back to the late 1800s. The creature was first spotted by two brothers, Joe and Charlie Francis, in 1891. According to the New England Folklore blog, a few months later, a hunting guide, named Clarence Duffy, was out in the woods near Bangor when he encountered the surprise of his life. There, before him, was a towering *immense* moose—thirteen feet tall, with antlers that spanned ten feet. Its fur was a solid white color. Duffy was an experienced guide, so he knew his moose. For the next several years, the creature was spotted in Norcross, Bangor, and, later, near the Roach River. At the turn of the century, a bicyclist was enjoying his day riding when, all of a sudden, he spotted a moose at the side of the road. The startling appearance scared him so much that he jumped off his bike and climbed a tree. He watched as the moose looked at the bike, investigated it, and then meandered back to the woods.

According to many local legends, hunters throughout Maine have gone into the woods and encountered a behemoth moose there. Sightings occurred near Lobster Lake in 1911 and in the woods in 1938. Several more sightings have occurred after that. Often, the moose is seen as hunters enter a clearing in the woods, hunting nearby animals. Suddenly, before them, in a spot where there had been no creature, stands a gargantuan beast that causes the hunters to pause in their tracks.

While many people believe the animal is purely a figment of the imagination, others think that there might be more to the story. The creature is purportedly eight feet tall (at least) and has giant antlers. The beast is twice the weight of a normal moose, weighing about 2,500 pounds to the trained eye. According to more Maine legend, a group of hunters near the Molunkus stream in Maine happened to be hunting one day when they shot a white moose. Knowing they had made quite a discovery, the hunters hung it from a tree to skin the next day, but, when they woke the following morning, the moose had disappeared…as if spirited off.

Perhaps the most interesting thing about the moose is not its size—moose are fairly large and impressive—or its height. Most eyewitnesses have stated that the creature is not your typical brown moose, but a white one (or "dirty white"). How a white moose might get into the woods is anyone's guess. Some scientists theorize that if such a beast was to, indeed, exist, it was probably a type of albino species, perhaps caused by mutated genes.

The Spectre Moose has been seen throughout the Pine Tree State, particularly in the northern section, where moose tend to roam.

A similar, massive, brown creature has also been reported there, with the last sighting occurring in 2002, when people in Franklin, Maine, claimed to have seen the moose. Days later, a local restaurant burned down, leading some to believe that the moose may appear right before a disaster.

While there is no scientific proof that such a creature exists, numerous people have claimed to seen it. No one has ever produced a photograph of the animal, but reports still occur to this day, more than a century after the first one. Does the moose have a genetic mutation that makes it albino? Maybe. Others suggest that moose reports are actually about one of several different moose suffering from a tick infestation. According to biologists, tick infestation may cause moose to itch and that regular itching will cause hair to break. This results in gray hair shafts showing—giving those infected a white appearance—so this may be a natural explanation. Pictures of such moose corroborate the ghostly appearance.

However, there are many who still believe that the moose is not the result of a natural reason, but a more supernatural one. So, the next time you are in the Maine woods, keep your eyes out for the white, or ghost, moose of Maine.

Creature of Willoughby Lake

Location: Willoughby Lake, Vermont
Type of Creature: Sea monster
Last Seen: 1960s
AKA: Willa, Willy

The History

Willoughby Lake, in Vermont, appears to be a peaceful and tranquil spot nestled between Mt. Hor and Mt. Pisgah. A lake carved by ancient glaciers that once dominated the area, it is a place where people vacation, try to steal a calming respite, and enjoy life. It is also an angler's paradise, loaded with a variety of fish, including rainbow trout, perch, and salmon.

The Mystery

However, it is also home to more than just sun-drenched shores and stocked fish. According to legend, the lake has been home to unique lake monster sightings since the mid-nineteenth century. Affectionately known as Willa or Willy, the sea monster has long been witnessed periodically and has become a part of local folklore.

The stories of the Willoughby Lake monster joined the public record on August 14, 1868. On that date, in the region's Caledonian newspaper, an article appeared telling the story of a twelve-year-old boy named Stephen Edmonds. Edmonds had been visiting the area, when he noticed a strange ripple on the water. He got closer and witnessed a giant snake in the water. Entering the lake, he managed to kill the snake by splitting it in two with a sickle. Following its death, measurements were taken of the creature, placing it at twenty-three feet in length—that was quite a lake snake, if ever there was one.

In the 1950s, tragedy struck the lake. It was reported that a man had perished there. Divers took to the water, looking for the body of the man. While trying to reach the bottom of the lake, where depths range up to 300 feet, the men noticed something peculiar. There was a large hole on the lake's floor (perhaps connecting this lake to nearby Crystal Lake, as rumors have suggested). Divers came close to the hole, but turned back when they supposedly saw various eight-foot-long eels swimming nearby.

In 1986, Audey Besse of Monmouth, New Jersey, became the next person to have an unusual encounter with the creature. While spending time on the lake, she gazed out upon the water and saw a large creature floating near the surface. It resembled the quintessential lake monster, complete with a variety of humps penetrating the surface. The creature appeared to be near a section known as Wheeler's Camp. Besse knew she had discovered firsthand proof of the monster and raced to get a camera, but it disappeared before she could return.

What the creature is remains a mystery. However, it appears that, at the very least, the lake may be home to a series of giant eels that have existed for centuries. While this may seem farfetched, some locals have noticed that eels (though much smaller) have been spotted at nearby waterways. Stocked with plenty to eat and a potential access to another lake, Willoughby Lake seems to be an ideal place for a creature waiting to make its next appearance.

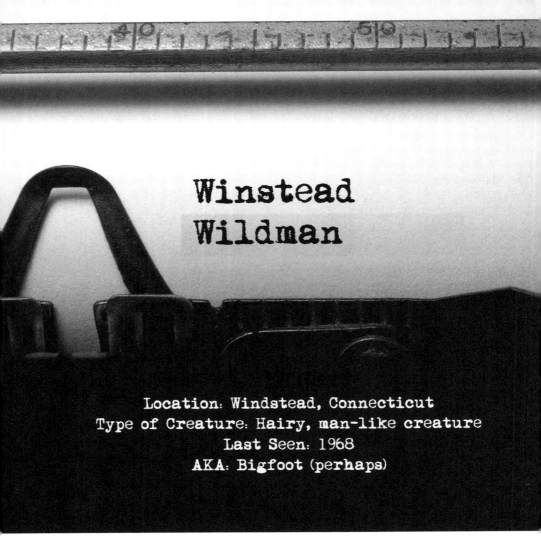

Winstead Wildman

Location: Windstead, Connecticut
Type of Creature: Hairy, man-like creature
Last Seen: 1968
AKA: Bigfoot (perhaps)

The History

Winstead, Connecticut (aka Winsted) is a quiet, docile part of the Constitution State. Situated in one of the largest expanses of non-highway sections in New England, Winstead is a relatively secluded and secure area.

The Mystery

In 1895, Winsted was the site of one of the more amazing creature sightings in Connecticut. On a balmy, sunny day, in the dog-days of August, local selectman Riley Smith had a strange encounter that brought much celebrity to the town.

It all started when Smith happened to be strolling along a wooded path with his dog. He noticed ripened berries and paused momentarily to collect them. All seemed right with the world when, suddenly, a large, hairy (and reportedly naked) man came bursting out of the woods. The Wildman, ranging possibly to nine feet tall, began crying wildly, moving rather unusually, and then ran straight back into the woods, disappearing into the summer air.

Riley was known as a stalwart of his day and also could be one to tell a tale or two. However, he appeared oddly overwhelmed by the incident— as was his trusted dog, known by many to be a fearless pooch, if ever there was one.

Riley's stories were soon corroborated by others. Several people reported the strange, hairy, man-like beast in the area. Before long, stories spread throughout the Northeast and many reporters flocked to the scene, hoping to find hide or hair of the strange being. After weeks of searching, nothing came up, so mystery hunters began searching for the creature, embarking on an old-fashion roundup, also to no avail....except for the strange stories told by locals.

The wildest story involved speculation that the Wildman was a man named Arthur Beckwith. According to area residents, Beckwith was a local artist who had been placed into a nearby asylum. He had escaped from a similar asylum in the past and was discovered sixth months later living in the woods of Cuba, gathering berries and nuts in order to survive, so this "man" was thought to be him, as well.

No one knows if the creature was indeed a man or not. After a lot of attention, the story quieted down and disappeared...that is, until 1968. In November of that year, a large creature, similar to the Wildman, was seen roaming the woods in nearby Litchfield. The report suggests it might have been a Bigfoot. Perhaps, instead, it was a descendent of the Wildman.

No other reports of the creature have been noted in recent times. However, it is worth mentioning that the area is surrounded by lots of trees. Although some of the underlying growth that would provide food has died off, there are plenty of wild berries, fruits, and nuts that could support a creature.

Woods Devil

Location: White Mountains
and Coos County, New Hampshire
Type of Creature: Tall, hairy biped
with gray skin and gray fur
Last Seen: 1990s
AKA: Bigfoot (perhaps)

The History

The woods of New England still teem with trees. Although the dense forests are not quite as filled as they once were, there is still a wide range of them throughout the region. These forests provide fertile ground for vegetation, abundant wildlife, and, quite frankly, more than a few unusual stories.

The legendary White Mountains is host to one of these stories. An area known for majestic mountains, beautiful fall foliage, and tourist spots, the mountains are also home to many legends. While most legends surround people and places, some involve curious creatures that roam the woods. Perhaps one of the best known of these is the tale of the Woods Devil.

The Mystery

Local legend has it that the woods of northern New England, including parts of the White Mountains and Coos County, New Hampshire, are home to a mysterious lot of creatures. This lot has been seen by various people who all report similar things. The creatures are tall and quite lanky, covered with fur, often described as brown or grey, with an almost human-like appearance (except for their faces). They tend to suddenly "show-up" when a person least expects it, often when hikers or naturalists are walking through the woods.

These mysterious creatures earned the nickname "Woods Devils" over time and were known for their wily ways. They would disappear quickly when a person saw them, almost dissolving into nothing behind a tree or other nearby vegetation. Sometimes these devils would make a sudden appearance, as if looking to see the specific person at the location, and then it would disappear.

People who have tried to approach them frequently became aware that the beasts were tentative and nervous. The Woods Devils did their best to keep distance between themselves and people and would find ways to block viewers' paths with trees. This way, the creatures might be gaining a sense of security.

The Woods Devils are also described as quick-witted. They seek escape routes, and if one is not present, eyewitnesses over the years claim that the creatures would wait until they were definitely seen by someone, and then unleash curdling calls that would make even the most experienced woodsmen run for cover.

In the 1930s, a rash of sightings of these devils were reported, but their presence seems to have dwindled over time. However, in recent years, these devils may have reemerged. According to the Natural Plane blogs, a creature was possibly located in the New Hampshire woods in the 1990s. An eyewitness happened to be taking pictures near the Androscoggin River at an impromptu photo shoot. A Woods Devil appeared in the woods, and then went back to hiding. The man attempted to find the creature, to no avail.

While these creatures may seem timid, local lore also says that they are not a force to be reckoned with. The screams they unleash should be taken as a stern warning to "stay clear." In fact, it is generally believed that if there are such beasts, it is best to give it a wide birth and move in a different direction. The Woods Devils quite possibly could be aggressive and it moves with great speed.

No one knows the true nature of what these speculative creatures might be. Some paranormal researchers believe that the Woods Devil might be a Bigfoot. However, many eyewitnesses claim that it has a less human and more humanoid appearance, which has lead some to believe that, perhaps, the Woods Devil—if it exists—might actually be a long-lost descendent of early man.

Appendix

List of New England Water Creatures

For those who are interested in searching or checking for water creatures, the following is a partial list of water bodies that are supposedly home to unknown water creatures.

Connecticut

Basile Lake

Connecticut River

Massachusetts

Twin Lakes

Silver Lake

Gloucester Bay

Maine

Boyden Lake

Casco Bay

Chain Lake

Machias Lake

Moosehead Lake

Lake Pohengamook

Sysladobsis Lake

Rangely Lake

Mount Desert Island Sea Serpent

Pocomoonshine Lake Monster

Saco River's White Money

New Hampshire

Lake Winnisquam

Moore Reservoir

Vermont

Lake Champlain

Connecticut River

Dead Creek

Lake Memphremagog

Winooski River

Willoughby Lake

Glossary

Bigcats Name given to large cats that grow in wild.

Biped Creature that walks on two feet.

Cryptid Animal that is of unexplained origin at the time it is spotted.

Crytozoologist A person who studies cryptids.

Feral A wild version of a typically domesticated animal, such as a cat or dog.

Fisher cat Large creature, related to the marten, that resembles a cross between a raccoon and a large black cat. It unleashes a bloodcurdling cry.

French and Indian War Series of wars in the seventeenth and eighteenth century between British settlers, French settlers, and Native Americans (who fought on both sides).

Ice Age A period of general climatic cooling throughout the world, which resulted in glacial sheets spreading from the Arctic and Antarctic regions.

Lightkeeper Person who is in charge of tending a lighthouse and keeping it in operation.

Northeast Kingdom Northeast corner of Vermont.

Picket's Night The night before Halloween, which proved popular with mischief makers.

Plesiosaur Prehistoric dinosaur that lived in the ocean and had a long neck; many sea serpents are thought to be plesiosaurs.

Prospector A person who looks for gems and mineral deposits, such as gold.

Sasquatch Native American name for Bigfoot.

Resources

Books

If you are truly interested in the curious creatures of New England, then here are a few must-reads. These books are terrific and were used throughout this text to provide information and support. They are well-written and really capture the imagination. Check them out.

Belanger, Jeff. *Weird Massachusetts: Your Travel Guide to Massachusetts' Local Legends and Best Kept Secrets*. New York, New York: Sterling, 2008.

Cahill, Robert Ellis. *New England's Marvelous Monsters*. Salem, Massachusetts: Chandler Smith, 1983.

Things That Go Bump In The Night. Salem, Massachusetts: Old Salt Box Co, 1989.

Citro, Joseph. *The Vermont Monster Guide*. Lebanon, New Hampshire: University Press of New England, 2009.

Weird New England: Your Travel Guide to New England's Local Legends and Best Kept Secrets. New York, New York: Sterling 2005.

Coleman, Loren et al. *Field Guide to Lake Monsters, Sea Monsters, and other Denizens of the Deep*. New York, New York: Tarcher, 2003.

Websites

The following sites are simply fabulous. They have been used throughout the research of this book and, as you can see, provide a wealth of information throughout. All of these sites are great for those who are interested in the supernatural and unexplained. I highly recommend them.

Cryptomundo

URL: http://www.cryptomundo.com

For anyone who wants to learn about cryptids and unusual creatures, this is the place to start. A wealth of great information—managed by Loren Coleman—this well-researched and documented website will give you all you'll ever need to know about cryptids...and more.

Damned Connecticut

URL: http://www.damnedct.com

As the site mentions, posting dedicated to all that is "weird, unexplained, and unusual in Connecticut." It has a variety of interesting information and is a great read.

Joseph Citro Blog

URL: http://josephacitro.blogspot.com

This site is maintained by Joseph Citro. While it has information about books, it also has some fun and interesting information about paranormal creatures of the Green Mountain State.

Massachusetts Paranormal Crossroads

URL: http://www.masscrossroads.com

Information on a variety of paranormal stories from Massachusetts. The stories are interesting and very unique.

New England Folklore Blog

URL: http://newenglandfolklore.blogspot.com

Great collection of all folklore of New England. It has a great assortment of paranormal, but it also contains a wealth of information about the lore, *and lure*, of New England.

Strange Maine

URL: http://strangemaine.blogspot.com

A creative and eclectic assortment of Maine stories can be found at this site. It is definitely a wonderful collection of the unique and unusual stories from Maine.

Other Resources

Besides the sites listed previously, these are specific Internet, television, newspaper, and other resources that were used to help gain information about certain topics. These sources provided valuable for specific creatures mentioned throughout this book.

Ap'cnic

"Nashoba Hill." Nashoba Hill: The Hill that Roars website. URL: http://www.boudillion.com/nashobahill/nashobahill.htm.

Nagog Pong. URL: http://findlakes.com/nagog_pond_massachusetts~ma00129.htm.

Bigfoot

Conway Daily Sun. November 24, 2006.

"Essex County Sightings." Gulf Coast Bigfoot Research Organization. URL: http://www.gcbro.com/MAessex001.html.

Grafton Bigfoot Encounter. Mid American Bigfoot Research Center forum. URL: http://mid-americanbigfoot.com/forums/viewtopic.php?f=72&t=360.

http://www.bigfootencounters.com/sbs/litchfield.htm.

"Litchfield Country Connecticut." URL: www.bigfootencounters.com.

"Litchfield Sighting." Gulf Coast Bigfoot Research Organization. URL: http://www.gcbro.com/CNlitch001.htm.

Luce, Patrick. "Could Bigfoot be Roaming Rhode Island?" *North Kingstown Patch*, October 24, 2011. Retrieved: http://northkingstown.patch.com/articles/could-bigfoot-be-roaming-rhode-island.

Malone, Michael. "Man Spots Bigfoot in Bennington County, Vermont." *Bennington Banner*, September 26, 2003. URL http://www. benningtonbanner.com/Stories/0,1413,104~8678~1657744,00.html. Also found at URL: http://www.bigfootencounters.com/articles/ bennington.htm.

"New England Outdoors Hiking—New England's Bigfoot." Sixstates.net. URL: http://www.sixstates.net/0808bigfoot.htm.

"October Mountain State Forest." North East Sasquatch Researchers Association. URL: http://www.teamnesra.net/forum/index. php?showtopic=569.

Parsons, Ed. "Hiking: Myth versus reality of Sasquatch in the Ossippee Range." *Conway Daily Sun*, Conway, New Hampshire.

"Report #1199." Bigfoot Field Research Association. URL: http://bfro.net/ GDB/show_report.asp?id=1199.

"Sasquatch in New England." The Bigfoot Field Research Organization. URL: http://www.bfro.net/NEWS/newengland.asp.

Black Cats

Prevo, Robert. The Black Panther: Fact or Folklore. URL: http://www. cryptozoology.com/articles/bigcats.php.

Black Flash

"Black Flash of Cape Cod." URL: http://blogs.forteana.org/node/130.

"Fall Brings Out Black Flash." *Provincetown Advocate,* October 26, 1939. Volume 70, Number 42. Page 1.

"Skully Joe." URL: http://www.whitings-writings.com/recipes/cod_pf1.htm. www.provincetownportuguesefestival.com/.../PortugueseFest2010.pdf.

Block Ness Monster

Arnold, Neil. "The Block Ness Monster." Still on the Track website. URL: http://webcache.googleusercontent.com/search?q=cache:635foGUWx1UJ:forteanzoology.blogspot.com/2009/04/guest-blogger-neil-arnold-block-ness.html+Block+Ness+Monster&cd=9&hl=en&ct=clnk&gl=us&client=firefox-a&source=www.google.com.

Morse, Carroll. "Creatures of Halloween II." Anchor Rising website. URL: http://www.anchorrising.com/barnacles/003501.html.

Cassie of Casco Bay

"Cassie: The Casco Bay Sea Serpent." Maine Mysteries blogspot. August 2, 2008.

Zwicker. Roxie. *Haunted Portland: From Pirates to Ghost Brides.* Charleston, South Carolina: The History Press, 2007.

Champ

Champmonster.com website. URL: http://champmonster.com/.

Clarke, Rod. " Vermont Folklore Builds on Champlain Monster." UPI story appearing in *Sarasota Herald*. December 25, 1975.

Cryptomundo website. URL: http://www.cryptomundo.com/cryptozoo-news/new-champ/.

Kluever, Michael H. "Sea Monsters or Myths." *The Milwaukee Journal*, October 7, 1980.

Chicken Easting Fish of Stratford Light

"Lordship Mermaids and Sea Creatures." Lordship Mermaid and Sea Creature website. URL: http://www.lordshiphistory.com/SEAMONSTERwebpage.html.

"Sea Monsters and Serpents, Long Island Sound." Damned Connecticut website. URL: http://www.damnedct.com/sea-monsters-serpents-long-island-sound/

"Stratford Point Lighthouse." New England Lighthouses website. URL: http://www.lighthouse.cc/stratford/history.html.

Connecticut's Black Dog

"The Black Dog of Meriden." Scary Stories for Kids website. URL: http://www.scaryforkids.com/meriden/.

"The Hanging Hills of Meriden: Legend and Geology." Connecticut Windows to the Natural World website. URL: http://cttrips.blogspot.com/2006/01/hanging-hills-of-meriden-legend.html.

Connecticut's River Monster

"Lordship Mermaids and Sea Creatures." Lordship Mermaid and Sea Creature website. URL: http://www.lordshiphistory.com/SEAMONSTERwebpage.html.

"Sea Monsters and Serpents, Long Island Sound." Damned Connecticut website. URL: http://www.damnedct.com/sea-monsters-serpents-long-island-sound/.

Dover Demon

"Dover Demon." American Monsters.com. URL: http://www.americanmonsters.com/site/2010/03/dover-demon-massachusetts-usa/.

"Dover Demon." Lost Tapes—Animal Planet. URL: http://animal.discovery.com/tv/lost-tapes/dover-demon/.

"Dover Demon." Wikipedia. URL: http://en.wikipedia.org/wiki/Dover_Demon.

Sullivan, Mark. "Decades later, the Dover Demon still haunts." *Boston Globe*, October 29, 2006. URL: http://www.boston.com/news/local/articles/2006/10/29/decades_later_the_dover_demon_still_haunts/.

Durham Gorilla

"Durham Gorilla Revisited." Cryptonmundo website. URL: http://www.cryptomundo.com/cryptozoo-news/durham-gorilla/.

"Thirty-Five Years Later: The Durham Gorilla." Strange Maine blogspot. URL: http://strangemaine.blogspot.com/2008/08/35-years-later-durham-gorilla.html.

Glastenbury Monster

"Bennignton Monster Mania." New England Folklore Blog. URL: http://newenglandfolklore.blogspot.com/2009/10/october-monster-mania-bennington.html.

Glawackus

"Beware the Fisher Cat." Damned Connecticut website. URL: http://www.damnedct.com/beware-the-fisher-cat/.

"The Glawackus." Damned in Connecticut website. URL: http://www.damnedct.com/the-glawackus-glastonbury/.

Hockomock Swamp Creature

"Hockomock Swamp." Haunted North America website. URL: http://www.hauntednorthamerica.com/hockomockswamp.htm.

"Hockomock Swamp." New England Paranormal Research. URL: http://webcache.googleusercontent.com/search?q=cache:KUWjlImO-I4J:www.neparanormalresearch.com/apps/forums/topics/show/1395969-hockomock-swamp-%3Fpage%3Dlast+hockomock+monster&cd=8&hl=en&ct=clnk&gl=us&client=firefox-a.

"Hockomock Swamp." Suite101. URL: http://mysterious-places.suite101.com/article.cfm/hockomock_swamp.

Muscato, Ross. A. "Tales From the Swamp: From Ape-like Creatures to Glowing Lights Hockomock has Kept its Secrets for Centuries." *Boston Globe*, October 30, 2005.

Memphre

"Memphre The Monster of Lake Memphremagog." Vermonter.com website. www.vermonter.com/nek/memphremyth.asp.

"Sea Monsters In Vermont" Secretary of State website. URL: http://www.sec.state.vt.us/kids/champ.html.

Pigman of Vermont

Levitt, Alice. "Local Legends." Seven Days website. URL: http://www.7dvt. com/2009local-legends.

Plum Island Kraken

"Dan Brown's Surprise: Giant Squid." Cryptomundo website. URL: http:// www.cryptomundo.com/cryptozoo-news/browns-squid/.

Levitt, Alice. "Local Legends." Seven Days website. URL: http://www.7dvt. com/2009local-legends.

Pinto, Nick. "Giant Squid Discovery Brings Back Memories of Plum Island's Squidly." *Gloucester Times*, March 6, 2007. URL: http://www. gloucestertimes.com/local/x645261294/Giant-squid-discovery-brings-back-memories-of-PIum-Islands-Squidly/print

"World's Largest Invertebrate." Ocean Planet website. URL: http://seawifs. gsfc.nasa.gov/OCEAN_PLANET/HTML/squid_Architeuthis.html.

Pomoola

"Bigfoot in Maine, Part 1." Strange Maine website. URL: http://strangemaine. blogspot.com/2008/10/bigfoot-in-maine-part-1.html.

"Historic Bigfoot Sightings: Maine." Bigfoot Encounter website. URL: http://www.bigfootencounters.com/sbs/campingout.htm.

Ponik

"Lake Monster Legend Lives on in Northern Maine." TV Station 6. WCSH, Portland.

"Ponik." Maine Mysteries website. URL: Mainemysteries.blogspot. com/2008/08/ponik.html. August 4, 2008.

"Ponik, the Monster of Lake Pohenegamook." Cryptozoo-oscity website. URL: http://cryptozoo-oscity.blogpot.com/2009/07/ponik-monster-of-lake-pohenegamook.html.

Provincetown Sea Monster

Miller, John and Tim Smith. *Cape Cod Stories: Tales from the Cape, Nantucket, and Martha's Vineyard.* San Francisco, California: Chronicle Books, 1996.

Pukwudgie

"Pukwudgies: Myth or Monster." Massachusetts Crossroads website. URL: http://www.masscrossroads.com/pukwudgies.

"The Pukwudgie." Pukwudgie.com website. URL: http://pukwudgie.com/.

Sidehill Gougers

"Fearsome Critters Online edition." Folklore Lumberwoods website. URL: http://www.folklore.lumberwoods.com/pg39.htm.

"Sidehill Gougers." Museum of hoaxes website. URL: http://www.museumofhoaxes.com/hoax/animals/comments/4357/

"The Wamphoofus—A Sad Evolutionary Tale." Nature Compass website. URL: http://nature.thecompass.com/gmcburlington/news/0410wamp.html.

Slipperyskin

Eberhart, George M. *Mysterious Creatures: A Guide to Cryptozoology,* Volume 1. Santa Barbara: California: ABC CLIO, 2002.

"Old Slipperyskin: Vermont's First Horror." Joseph Citro Blog. URL: http://josephacitro.blogspot.com/2010_01_22_archive.

Wheeler, Scott. "Slipperyskin: Bear, Bigfoot, or Indian." Vermonter.com website. URL: http://www.vermonter.com/northlandjournal/slipperyskin.asp.

Springheel Jack

"Springheel Jack Sightings." Unknown Creatures.com. URL: http://www.unknown-creatures.com/springheel-jack.html.

"Springheel Jack: Top Ten Bizarre Cryptids." URL: http://listverse.com/2010/07/25/top-10-bizarre-cryptids/.

Thunderbirds

"Legend of the Giant Bird." URL: http://sped2work.tripod.com/giantbird. html.

"The Origin of the Thunderbird." First People, the Legends website. URL: http://www.firstpeople.us/FP-Html-Legends/TheOriginoftheThunderbird-Passamaquoddy.html.

"The Thunderbird of New England." Strange New England website. URL: http://www.strangene.com/monsters/bird.htm.

Turner Creature

LaFlamme, Mark. "Like the Horns of a Devil." *Sun Journal.* August 17, 2006.

"Maine's Dog Killer." Crytomundo website November 16, and 18, 2005. URL: http://www.foxnews.com/story/2006/08/16/maine-mystery-beast-possibly-killed-by-car/

"Strange Mutant Found Dead in Maine." *Associated Press*, August 16, 2005. URL: (for November 16) http://www.cryptomundo.com/cryptozoo-news/maines-dog-killing-hyena/
(for November 18) http://www.cryptomundo.com/cryptozoo-news/maines-dog-killer-cont/

Ware Swamp Monster

"Not Ware's Pet Alligator." *New York Times*. July 4, 1922. Retrieved URL: http://query.nytimes.com/mem/archive-free/pdf?res=F40813F739551A738DDDAD0894DF405B828EF1D3.

White Moose

"Ghost Moose." Trek Nature website. URL: http://www.treknature.com/gallery/photo148971.htm.

"King Moose." Crytomundo website. URL: http://www.cryptomundo.com/cryptozoo-news/king-moose/.

"The Spectre Moose." Museum of Hoaxes website. URL: http://www. museumofhoaxes.com/hoax/weblog/comments/the_specter_moose.

"The Spectre Moose of Maine." New England Folklore blogspot. URL: http://newenglandfolklore.blogspot.com/2012/03/specter-moose-of-maine.html.

Willoughby Lake Creature

Fisher, Harriet F. *Willoughby Lake Legends and Legacies.* Rutland, Vermont: Academy Books, 1988.

"Lake Willoughby Creature a Giant Eel?" Croptozoo-oscity Blog. March 11, 2010. URL: http://cryptozoo-oscity.blogspot.com/2010/03/lake-willoughby-creature-giant-eel.html.

"Vermont Legends, Hauntings, and Ghost Stories." Vermonter.com website. URL: http://www.vermonter.com/weird-vermont.asp.

Winstead Wildman

"Wildman Craze of 1895 Made Thing a Little Hairy." *Waterbury Republican American*, July 14, 2002. As found at BFRO website. URL: http://bfro. net/GDB/show_article.asp?id=310.

Wood's Devil

"Coos County, New Hampshire Wood Devils." Bigfoot Encounters website. URL: http://www.bigfootencounters.com/sbs/coos.htm.

"New Hampshire Woods Devil." Natural Planes Blogspot. URL: http:// naturalplane.blogspot.com/2011/09/new-hampshire-wood-devils.html.

"Water Creatures." URL: http://www.worldlingo.com/ma/enwiki/en/ Lake_monster#Massachusetts.

Varied

http://www.etravelmaine.com/attractions/strange-maine/maine-sea-monsters/

Index